# What People Are Saying About GINA MARIE HAMILTON and *Healing* Beyond the Hurt

"I was feeling really depressed and alone. I felt broken. But knowing that there was someone out there willing to talk to me, to comfort me, meant the world. I'm so grateful for Gina's support. Thank you, Gina, for calming me down."

—Z.K.

"Gina, you took what I had and helped me get through it. You gave me resources for the future and that made me feel like I deserve one. You're meant to help people, thank you."

—A.B.

"I wasn't really sure where this would go. But, Gina, you've given me a spark of courage. I will do this. Thank you!"

—B.H.

"I loved this! I'm no longer scared. This was great!"

—K.D.L.

"Thank you! I'm going to keep trying for the care I know I need even when it's scary."

—S.H.

"Gina, you helped me calm down and make it manageable."
—C.B.

"Thank you so much for uplifting me. Keep up the great work!"
—G.H.

"Thank you so much for helping me. I definitely feel better about myself and what I'm dealing with. Thanks for making me feel safe."
—D.O.

"Gina, thank you. Talking to you kept me from thinking bad thoughts and you gave me information that I can use. You are truly an angel."
—R.W.E.

"Gina, you were incredibly helpful and super patient with me. You understood where I was coming from and did not judge me. You gave me great resources that I have not seen before, so it was super helpful. I went into the conversation feeling incredibly low and came out not crying anymore and content with next steps. Thank you!"
—J.T.

"You saved me in more ways than one."
—O.H.L.

"Thanks for being there when I felt completely alone."
—M.J.H.

"Gina is amazing. She made me feel infinitely better about my situation."
—K.L.T.

# Healing Beyond the Hurt

## TURNING TRAUMA INTO TRIUMPH

**GINA MARIE HAMILTON**

HEALING BEYOND THE HURT

*Turning Trauma into Triumph*

Copyright © 2026. Gina Marie Hamilton. All rights reserved. No part of this publication may be reproduced, distributed, or transmitted in any form or by any means, including photocopying, recording, or other electronic or mechanical methods, without the prior written permission of the publisher, except in the case of brief quotations embodied in critical reviews and certain other noncommercial uses permitted by copyright law.

For permission requests, speaking inquiries, and information on the course, *Finding Direction from Within*, email gina@ginahamiltoncoaching.com.

Gina Marie Hamilton
2081 Harrodsburg Road #1079
Lexington, KY 40504
**bodyelementsmindelevation.com**

Edited by Lori Lynn Enterprises | LoriLynnEnterprises.com
Designed by Transcendent Publishing | TranscendentPublishing.com

ISBN: 979-8-9941688-5-1

Disclaimers: Please note that due to the sensitive nature of their stories, identifying names have been adapted to protect the privacy of each individual. The contents of this book is provided on an "as-is" basis and is not meant to exclude information and treatment from your medical providers. The information provided in this book is for informational purposes only and is not intended to diagnose, treat, cure, or prevent any condition or disease. The author disclaims all representations and warranties, including but not limited to warranties of healthcare (including mental health) for a particular purpose. No assumption of responsibility is accepted by the author for errors, inaccuracies, omissions, or any other inconsistencies herein. Readers should consult with their normal licensed provider and seek medical support when facing a mental health crisis. Your use of the information in this book is at your own discretion and of your own choosing.

"Only when we are brave enough to explore the darkness will we discover the infinite power of our light."

—Brené Brown

# CONTENTS

Dedication . . . . . . . . . . . . . . . . . . . . . . . . . . . . ix

Surviving Trauma . . . . . . . . . . . . . . . . . . . . . . . . 1

1 | From Shattered to Whole: Reclaiming Your Power . . . . . . 11

2 | Voices Unheard, Strength Unseen: Owning Your Story . . . . 17

3 | The Healing Within: Embracing Your Inner Warrior . . . . . . 27

4 | The Strength in Vulnerability: Embracing Your True Self . . . 35

5 | Shedding the Past: Releasing What No Longer Serves You . . . . 43

6 | The Power of "No": Setting Boundaries with Love . . . . . . . 51

7 | Boundaries as Bridges: Building Safe Spaces for Healing . . . 59

8 | Sacred Self-Care: Nurturing Your Mind, Body, and Soul . . . 67

9 | The Path to Peace: Forgiving Yourself and Others . . . . . . . 75

10 | Empathy as a Superpower: Healing Through Compassion . . .81

11 | Rewriting Your Narrative: Becoming the Hero of Your Story .87

12 | Finding Your Voice: Speaking Your Truth with Confidence  93

13 | The Art of Letting Go: Freeing Yourself from the Past . . . . 99

14 | Rising from the Ashes: The Phoenix Within . . . . . . . . . .105

15 | Turning Scars into Stars: The Art of Transformation . . . . .113

16 | Redefining Yourself: Beyond the Pain . . . . . . . . . . . . . . .117

17 | From Surviving to Thriving: Creating Your New Normal . .123

18 | The Power of Choice: Creating the Life You Deserve . . . .129

19 | Unbroken: The Journey to Self-Love. . . . . . . . . . . . . . .135

20 | Living in Your Power: Embracing Your Future with Grace .141

A Note from Me to You. . . . . . . . . . . . . . . . . . . . . . . . .147

Acknowledgments. . . . . . . . . . . . . . . . . . . . . . . . . . . .149

About the Author . . . . . . . . . . . . . . . . . . . . . . . . . . . .151

Step Into Your Power . . . . . . . . . . . . . . . . . . . . . . . . . .155

Connect with Gina . . . . . . . . . . . . . . . . . . . . . . . . . . .157

# DEDICATION

To my sons, Kaden and Carter, who have shown me the true beauty of life and an everlasting love without condition. There are not enough words that will ever express how proud I am of you. Always remember, I love you both.

# SURVIVING TRAUMA

It was 6:00 a.m. when the blaring sound of the alarm jolted Harper from her restless daze. Her head throbbed with the ache of countless sleepless nights. She barely had the energy to crack open her eyes, and when she did, the sight in her bedside mirror was almost startling.

Her once-loose curls were a tangled mess, the strands matted together from where tears had soaked them into submission. The remnants of black mascara streaked her cheeks like war paint, contrasting against the faded pink of her favorite "You Can Do It!" t-shirt, which now felt more like a cruel reminder than a source of inspiration. Her unicorn socks—quirky, comforting, and now slightly mismatched—peeked out from beneath the blanket.

Her mind was a freeway of chaos. Thoughts zoomed past, each one more exhausting than the last. *"What did I even do yesterday? Did I eat? Is it Tuesday? Saturday?"*

She squeezed her temples, trying to quiet the roar of racing worries and replayed drama that refused to release her from its grip. Her brain felt like it had been on overdrive for days—weeks, even—but somehow, the nighttime made it crueler. Every moment of doubt, shame, and anger echoed louder in the silence.

The alarm shrilled again, cutting through her spiraling thoughts. Harper groaned, her arm flopping over to smack the snooze button. Just five more minutes—though she knew five would become fifteen, and fifteen might become the entire morning if she allowed it.

Her body sank back into the three pillows behind her. She pulled the comforter over her head like a shield against the world. Beneath its cocoon, the thought crept in: *"Maybe I'll be able to do this some other day. Just not today."* She let out a deep, shaky sigh.

The clock ticked on, but time felt meaningless. Harper considered calling into work. Her brain cycled through potential excuses. *"Migraine? Maybe stomach flu? Do I even need an excuse at this point?"* she thought bitterly, feeling like a hollow version of herself.

The sound of her snooze alarm jerked her out of her musings. This time, she didn't silence it right away. She stared at the glowing red numbers on her bedside clock, her mind swirling with an odd mix of guilt and dread. She felt stuck, like she was drowning in a sea of exhaustion but unable to call for help. "I can't keep doing this," she whispered, her voice barely audible even to herself.

Something stirred within her—a tiny flicker, like a faint ember buried deep in ashes. She didn't recognize it as hope just yet, but it was something. As she lay there, a memory of her favorite quote floated to the surface of her thoughts: "One small step at a time."

It wasn't much, but it was something she could cling to. She forced herself to sit up, the blanket sliding from her shoulders. The air felt cold against her tear-streaked face, but she didn't retreat back into bed. She stared at her reflection again, this time with a slight furrow of determination.

"Just one step," she muttered, planting her feet on the floor. It felt monumental, like climbing a mountain. But it was enough for now. "Maybe I'll commit to bed rot some other time."

## Taking the First Step

You are not broken. You are not beyond repair. Beneath the weight of your pain, there lies an unshakable strength, a light that has never dimmed, no matter how dark your world may have become. It's this light, this unwavering part of you, that I'm here to help you find, nurture, and let shine brighter than ever before.

Trauma has a way of wrapping itself around us, seeping into the corners of our hearts and minds, until it feels like there is no escape. It can make the world seem like a cold, unforgiving place—a place where pain overshadows joy, where fear takes root, and where hope is something distant and almost forgotten. If you've felt this way, I want you to know that you are not alone.

The darkness that trauma creates is real, and its impact can be devastating. It can rob us of our sense of safety, our confidence, our ability to trust others, and even our ability to trust ourselves. It can leave us feeling isolated, lost, and disconnected from the life we deserve. But even in this darkness, there is a light within you that never goes out. This light is your strength, your resilience, your power—the essence of who you truly are.

This book is your companion on the journey to reclaiming that light and letting it guide you to a life of fulfillment, peace, and joy. I understand the weight of what you carry. I know the deep ache of feeling unseen, unheard, and misunderstood. I've been there too, and I've come out the other side. I'm here to walk this path with you, to help you heal beyond the hurt, and to show you that your pain does not define you. Your story is not over; in fact, it's just beginning.

Together, we'll explore the depths of your pain, not to dwell there, but to understand it, honor it, and ultimately, transform it. We'll uncover the truth of your strength, the beauty in your resilience, and the power that lies in your ability to rise above the hurt. You are not broken—you are healing. You are not alone—I am here with you, every step of the way.

As you turn each page of this book, I want you to feel the warmth of unconditional love surrounding you. I want you to feel seen, heard, and valued, not just by me, but by yourself. You matter. Your story matters. Your healing matters. And most importantly, the life that you truly deserve and desire is not just a dream—it is within your reach.

This journey won't be easy, but it will be worth it. By the time you finish this book, I hope you'll see the incredible strength that has always been within you. I hope you'll feel empowered to take the actionable steps needed to create the life you've always dreamed of. And I hope you'll know, without a doubt, that you are deserving of all the love, joy, and peace that this life has to offer.

So, let's begin this journey together. Let's heal beyond the hurt and turn your trauma into triumph. The life you desire is waiting for you, my dear, and you are more than ready to claim it.

At the end of every chapter, you will be provided with an actionable step that is meant to help you on your path to healing. This is where those begin. Your first actionable step is as follows:

Reflect on your own story. Write down a few sentences about what brought you to this book and what you hope to gain from it.

I am interested in hearing about what drew you to my book. If you are interested in sharing your thoughts and feelings with me, please feel free to reach out and connect with me at gina@gina-hamiltoncoaching.com. I would love to hear from you. I will also send you a response back.

## This Book Is For ...

This book is for anyone who has ever experienced pain, loss, or trauma and is ready to heal and reclaim their power. It is for the brave souls who are tired of feeling stuck in their past and want to break free from the emotional wounds that have been holding them back. Whether you've been through abuse, heartbreak, betrayal, or personal struggles, *Healing Beyond the Hurt: Turning Trauma into Triumph* will guide you through the process of transforming your pain into power.

It is for:

- **Survivors of Abuse:** Whether it's physical, emotional, or psychological abuse, this book will help you heal from the scars of your past and show you how to build a life of peace, safety, and empowerment.
- **Women Who Have Experienced Trauma:** For women who have faced trauma, this book offers a compassionate roadmap for rediscovering your worth, reclaiming your voice, and living a life of confidence and self-love.
- **Medical Professionals:** Nurses, doctors, and healthcare workers who have witnessed traumatic events on the front lines and need tools for emotional healing will find solace and strength in these pages.
- **First Responders:** Police officers, firefighters, EMTs, and others who serve their communities often carry the weight of trauma from the emergencies they respond to.

This book provides the space to process that trauma and learn how to care for yourself emotionally.

- **Caregivers:** Those who care for loved ones, patients, or clients may find themselves emotionally drained and carrying the trauma of others. This book will teach you how to prioritize your healing while continuing to care for those who need you.
- **Survivors of Loss:** For anyone who has faced the overwhelming grief of losing a loved one, this book will help you find peace, healing, and the courage to move forward.
- **Anyone Feeling Stuck in the Past:** If you feel trapped by old wounds and emotional scars, this book will show you how to release the weight of your past and step into a future filled with possibility.
- **Therapists and Counselors:** Mental health professionals will benefit from the healing insights provided, which can also serve as a resource to share with clients working through trauma.
- **Military Veterans:** For those who have served and carry the weight of trauma from combat or service, this book offers a pathway to healing, reclaiming your sense of self, and finding peace in your new normal.
- **Teachers and Educators:** Educators who work with children impacted by trauma can benefit from understanding their own emotional health while navigating the challenges of supporting their students' healing journeys.

This book will show you how to turn your pain into power, break free from limiting beliefs, and rebuild your life on a foundation of strength and resilience, so that you can create a life of joy, purpose, and peace without allowing your past to control your future or define your worth.

If you're ready to let go of the hurt and embrace a life of triumph, this book is for you. Let's begin your healing journey together.

## Who Is Gina Marie Hamilton?

I wasn't always the woman you see before you today—a woman of strength, resilience, and purpose. There was a time when I felt broken, unworthy, and unsure of who I really was.

I faced struggles that cut deeply. Abuse, betrayal, the kind of pain that sinks its claws into you and leaves marks no one else can see. I tried to outrun it, to hide behind a facade of strength, but the truth was, I was lost. Life as I knew it crumbled, leaving me to pick up the pieces. Nothing would remain the same. I had to rebuild, brick by brick, from the ground up.

An attorney once handed me a pamphlet on domestic violence and told me to call "if I needed help." I did need help, but in the times that I truly needed help, I was not able to put the situation on hold and call the number on the pamphlet. I felt so let down by the system and my very valid concerns were ignored. I felt discarded and not cared for—much like my traumas had already repeatedly made me feel.

My life was once a battlefield, filled with villains lurking in the shadows of my mind and heart. These villains were not just people; they were the memories, fears, and beliefs that kept me chained to my past. But the moment I chose to confront those demons, everything began to shift.

The transformation began in those darkest moments, the times when I wanted to give up but didn't. I knew deep down that the only way forward was to face the pain head-on.

Along the way, I encountered incredible mentors and guides who became my North Star. They were not always people. Some were books, moments of clarity, or even a glimpse of sunlight filtering through the trees on a day I desperately needed hope. Slowly but surely, I learned to wield my pain like a sword, cutting away the chains that held me back.

There were roadblocks at every turn. My past kept calling me back, whispering that I wasn't good enough, that I couldn't possibly overcome all I had been through. But I kept pushing forward, fueled by a fire inside me that grew stronger with each step. I realized that every roadblock was an opportunity to prove just how much I could overcome.

As I faced the battles of my life, I started to achieve things I once thought impossible. I rebuilt my confidence, stepped into my power, and found a love for myself that was once hidden behind years of doubt.

I worked my way up the ladder from a Medical Assistant to a Registered Nurse—MSN (with 21 years of overall health care experience), launched a successful podcast, and found my calling as a Trauma Informed Health and Wellness coach who helps women heal from their past. I became a voice for those who have been silenced, and in doing so, I found my own voice.

I didn't stop there. My journey led me to victories I never imagined. I created courses, wrote guides, and built a community of women who, like me, were ready to turn their pain into power. I returned home from my journey, not as the same woman who had left, but as someone transformed, someone with magic to share.

Now, I'm here to ignite that same transformation in you. The magic potion I've brought back is this book, filled with the tools and wisdom you need to begin your own journey of healing and empowerment. You see, the power to change your life has been within you all along—you just need to uncover it. Together, we will face the villains of your past, confront the roadblocks in your present, and journey toward a future that is rich with possibility.

So here I am, extending my hand to you, ready to walk beside you as you ignite the flames of your own transformation. The road ahead won't be easy, but I promise, it will be worth it. You, too, can emerge victorious, living a life beyond the hurt and filled with triumph.

## What Does It Mean to Heal Beyond the Hurt and Turn Trauma into Triumph?

*Healing Beyond the Hurt: Turning Trauma into Triumph* is more than just a phrase—it's a powerful process of reclaiming your life from the pain of your past and stepping into a future built on strength, resilience, and self-love. It's about taking the scars left by trauma and turning them into symbols of triumph. But most importantly, it's about rewriting your story in a way that empowers you, allowing you to fully embrace your healing journey.

Why is this important? Healing from trauma isn't just about "getting over it." It's about *transforming* that pain into something meaningful and powerful—a stepping stone rather than a stumbling block. It's the difference between surviving and *thriving*. This book isn't just about surviving the hurt; it's about rising from the ashes, claiming your power, and becoming the hero of your story.

What makes my approach unique is how I fuse empathy, my lived experience, and actionable steps into a deeply personal and guided transformation. I understand trauma not just from a textbook perspective, but because I have lived it. I know the weight of the darkness, but I also know the beauty of finding the light. My originality comes in how I guide you through this journey: with warmth, strength, and a firm belief that every woman has the ability to turn her pain into power.

I don't offer cookie-cutter solutions. My approach digs deep into the root causes of your trauma, but more importantly, it empowers you to rebuild in a way that feels authentic to who you are. This book is your roadmap to creating lasting change by helping you build confidence, self-worth, and the tools to live victoriously.

To execute this transformation quickly, the most important step is simple: *believe in your ability to change.* Once you commit to seeing yourself as more than your trauma, everything else will follow. You have the power within you to rise, and together, we'll bring it to the surface.

If you're ready to dive deeper and ignite your personal transformation, I invite you to reach out and connect with me directly. You don't have to do this alone—I'm here to help guide you every step of the way. Reach out to me via email at gina@ginahamiltoncoaching.com, and let's embark on this journey to turn your pain into power. You *deserve* the life you've always dreamed of—let's make it happen.

# 1 | FROM SHATTERED TO WHOLE: RECLAIMING YOUR POWER

> *"When you can tell your story and it doesn't make you cry, you know you have healed."*
>
> —Karen Salmansohn

You never forget the moment when the world as you knew it shatters into a thousand pieces. The weight of trauma is a darkness that seems endless, suffocating in its depth, leaving you wondering if you'll ever feel the warmth of light again.

It's in this darkness that you may have found yourself sitting, lost and broken, questioning how you can possibly rebuild from the wreckage. But even in the deepest shadows, a small, steady light remains—your inner strength, your resilience, your power.

As you begin to accept the path to healing, that light starts to grow, guiding you toward reclaiming the life that is rightfully yours. It's a journey not of forgetting, but of transforming, of piecing together those shattered fragments into something even more beautiful, even more whole.

Here in these pages, you are seen, you are heard, you are valued. You are not alone in this. Together we will navigate this path hand in hand, with warmth, empathy, and unconditional love, as you reclaim the power that has always been yours.

If you're anything like me, you probably thought you had your whole life together in a neatly wrapped package, but that package has now become the gift you never wanted to receive.

You find yourself wrestling with so many emotions—fear, guilt, shame, peace, hope, hate, numbness, happiness, freedom—they are all a mixture now as you struggle to find your way.

Your mind may be filled with doubt and an endless array of questions. It's hard to know where to even begin now that your world has been turned upside down. When everything that you once knew is gone—even who you thought you were—how can you trust yourself to put things back together?

When everything has fallen apart in such a major way, it's not uncommon to question your own existence with thoughts like:

> "How am I going to get through this struggle when I never expected it?"
>
> "How do I pick up the pieces that are left to create a picture that I can truly see?"
>
> "I have no idea even where to begin."

The beginning of your healing journey requires you to do what you have already started to do: sit and think. Only it's not that simple. The healing journey requires you to sit and think *in your pain*.

Eek and cringe! I know, right?

No one wants to sign up to sit in any kind of pain unless they know that there is a reward on the other end. That's the thing—there *is* a reward on the other end—it's the healthy and healed version of yourself.

When you see that sitting in your pain and processing your emotions changes the way that you see things, your mindset and perspective shifts. No longer do you wade in despair.

Instead, you begin to create small, actionable steps to create a future that you love and are proud of. Processing through your pain delivers the one thing that you are desperately seeking—the version of you that is no longer shattered, but whole.

It's an understatement to say that sitting in your pain is painful. At times, it can be downright harsh, miserable, overwhelming, and depressing. But you must care enough about yourself to make changes as you seek a different and more positive way to live; otherwise, you wouldn't have opened this book.

When you allow yourself time to heal, the weight on your shoulders starts to feel lighter. When you notice this start to change, you can more readily take the time to process your emotions, acknowledge them, then set them free.

It's almost like when you were a kid holding the string of a balloon in your hand. You held tightly to the string because you did not want to lose the balloon—you fought to hold onto it.

Trauma is different—it's the balloon that you are fighting to let go of. Letting go of the string of this balloon frees you, changes you, and creates the version of you that has always existed beneath your clenched fist.

Exposing the darkness of your traumas will bring you into the light. With each bout of darkness you face, you start to gain clarity, hope, and acceptance for a brighter tomorrow. You realize the things that you have been made to believe about yourself are not true as you step forward to learn who you really are.

The light of exposed trauma brings about your courage, resilience, and bravery to create a new path that you have never once explored—the path that leads to a whole new you.

With time, you'll even discover traits and tools that have been present in your life, but you have chosen to ignore—traits and tools like self-love, self-confidence, self-acceptance, and self-worth. They all start with the word "self" because you cannot get them from anyone else.

You have started your journey with tons of questions that require answers. You think that the answers that you seek only exist in what others think and know about you, but the thing you have failed to realize is that the answers you seek lie within you.

This inner work will bring up all kinds of questions. This is normal. When you take the time to sit, reflect, and be silent, the answers will arrive to you like the sun on a crisp autumn day.

Your worries, struggles, and disbelief fall from you like leaves from the trees. The air around you feels fresh, breathable, and pure instead of stagnant, old, and full of fear.

Overcoming your trauma is a gift that you give to yourself—every day—and it's a gift that continues to provide you with the rewards of your efforts.

How much effort are you willing to put in to find the version of yourself that is whole and no longer shattered? If you have ever learned to drive a manual vehicle, then you know that learning that skill takes time, patience, and acceptance of failure.

There is no doubt that at some point you will stall the vehicle at the red light—this is part of the learning experience. It is the same way for healing from trauma and turning your pain into power.

You will stall at times. You will feel like you have failed. You will question why you are on the journey when things get harder before they become easier (this is normally because you are about to overcome your trauma and have a breakthrough of clarity). You will stumble and trip before you walk again with ease.

The important thing to realize here is that this is all a part of the journey. If it was simple, everyone would be doing it. Most choose to run and hide from the pain so they do not have to face it. They do not realize that this only prolongs the pain and makes it harder to face.

However, you are different. You are choosing to embark on a new path that has been created by you. It is ok to not feel ok at times. It is ok to think you have it figured out, only to realize that you need to start all over again.

On this path, you will start over several times, and with each time this occurs, you'll learn to embrace yourself and the process even more. It is never too late to start over.

Ask yourself, "Am I willing to stay stalled at the red light, or do I want to step forth and create a new path that I have never traveled before?" If you're ready to step forth and create a new path, welcome to the start of your journey, where the things that were once unknown to you become known in the most beautiful of ways.

This is your moment to shine and embrace the light that has burned continuously within you, even through your darkest of days. Wherever you are reading this—in the car, at home, in the bathtub—just know that I am sitting with you and joining you on your journey. Your journey awaits its creator—YOU.

## Actionable Step

Write a letter to your future self, expressing your commitment to reclaiming your power and beginning your healing journey.

This is a reminder to state what feels right to you without feeling the need to filter your words. You are writing this to yourself only, unless you decide to share it with someone else. It does not need to be perfect.

# 2 | VOICES UNHEARD, STRENGTH UNSEEN: OWNING YOUR STORY

*"If you feel unseen and unheard, create your own lane."*

—Robin S. Baker

There is a unique pain in the silence that follows trauma—the silence that holds your truth captive, echoing in the emptiness of your own mind. You may have kept quiet out of fear, out of the paralyzing dread that your voice would be dismissed, your pain minimized, or worse, that you wouldn't be believed at all.

The weight of unspoken words, the burden of secrets too heavy to carry alone, can make you feel isolated, as though the world has turned its back on your suffering. In the quiet of your own thoughts, you replay the hurt, the disbelief, and the crushing loneliness that comes from being unheard. But even in this silence, your story has power.

Your voice, though quiet now, carries the strength to heal, to reclaim your truth, and to shatter the chains of fear that have kept you from speaking out.

Here in these pages, you are not alone. I see you, I hear you, and I am here to remind you that your story matters. Together, we will find the courage to break the silence, to share your truth, and to reclaim the power that lies within your voice.

How many times have your thoughts from the past been on replay? At this point, I am sure that you have lost count as you try to grasp and process what has happened to you. This can be an overwhelming task to take on as you try to balance a normal life outside of your mind.

What is normal, anyways? After trauma has been a part of your life, there isn't just one solid way to define it. Things are as they are, and you start to realize that you have no control over what happens to you. Or do you?

Part of healing from trauma is the ability to rewrite your story with a new ending that is satisfying to your heart, mind, and soul. Eventually, you will have to get comfortable enough to break your silence and speak your truth—the story of what happened to you.

You may have been brave enough to speak your truth before, with hope in your heart that someone would finally be there to comfort you. Only that's not what happened at all. Instead, you were met with negative statements, dismissive remarks, and instead of the person taking responsibility for causing the trauma in the first place, the blame was placed on you.

I am sorry that you were not provided with a safe space of comfort, love, and validation. The support you needed was not there when you needed it most. Rest assured that the support that you need, when you need it most, is written in the pages of this book. No longer are you alone on your journey. I am here with you.

If you've already been courageous enough to break your silence, I commend you. This is something that is very difficult to do in the beginning, but once you start, you gain traction and it becomes that much easier to speak your truth moving forward.

If you have not broken your silence yet, this is an opportune time to start getting comfortable with breaking it. Your story may not come out loudly; it may come out in writing or as a whisper as you question yourself each day.

It is your choice to make about how and when you will break your silence. Just because someone else says negative things about your story, that does not mean that your story didn't happen.

Despite what other people may say, what you've experienced still affected you, changed you, and created the darkness that you so often sit alone in today. The only validation you need is your own belief in your story.

People can only meet you where they have met themselves. If they have never experienced trauma or sat in their own pain from it, their ability to sit with you is quite low. This is also ok. Continue to believe in yourself and share your truth.

When you start the journey of breaking your silence, you'll notice that your mind will play some cruel tricks on you. You'll question if what you are stating really happened, if now is a good time to share, and if anyone will believe you. This is all normal, but it is also a side effect of the traumas that you experienced.

Somewhere along the way you have been made to believe that you need to stay small and silent. Sharing your story is the exact opposite. It's freeing and allows you to grow in the direction that you choose.

Freeing your mind from these tricks can be as simple as stating your thoughts out loud and listening to your own words. This will clear your mind and allow you to hear that what is going through your mind is not true at all, so you can continue on the path.

You will experience heightened anxiety and nervousness when you decide to share your story, whether by sharing it with someone else or by simply journaling it so you can read it.

There is no wrong way to choose to share your story—it can be done in countless ways. Examples are: sharing it with a trusted friend, opening up about what has happened on a crisis line, journaling, or even a support group. If you have a family member that you trust, that can be another option. However you choose, it needs to be comfortable enough that you want to share.

I can remember when I started to put the pieces of my own traumas together. I am definitely not a stranger to trauma in my life, and I have had to learn to find small actionable solutions to turn my pain into power.

I started to share my story quietly by journaling. I did not speak to anyone about it for a really long time, mostly because I was still trying to understand it myself. If someone were to ask me questions about it, I knew that I would not be able to answer them, because I simply just did not know.

I journaled for years until I noticed that I needed another way. Journaling was no longer helping me. I decided to locate a support group, because I had tried therapy before and it just was not the right fit for me. I needed something new.

This is when I found the support groups in Sharewell. I was nervous and even fearful that when I did share, I would not be believed … again. I had already shared and was not believed or supported.

The alienation that I felt was tremendous. I did not want to go through that again, and that was the reason why I fell silent again: in my silence, I felt protected and believed. At this point, I knew I needed to step forward on my healing journey—it was now being required of me. I went to a few sessions and was only able to state my name, where I was from, and how I felt … kinda.

I realized that I was dissociating when I talked in an effort to protect myself even more. I continued to be patient and reassure myself that I was safe and that it was ok for me to share my story. Maybe I would be able to help others.

Finally, I was able to share. It was not planned. I just felt comfortable enough to be able to share part of what I had been through. At first, the amount of care and concern from others in the session who had experienced what I had been through was overwhelming.

It took me a couple of days to process and realize that there were others like me in the world. I had battled alone for years by myself while trying to keep my life together, but thankfully, I was no longer alone on my journey.

After finally feeling safe enough to share my story, I started to connect with others on a deeper level. This is the type of connection that I had always wanted.

I made the choice to create my own Sharewell sessions and to become a host. I created two separate Sharewell sessions that I hosted at different times. My first one was called "Dissociation Is a Superpower" since I had been learning about my tendency to dissociate when I felt unsafe.

I realized that when I was dissociating, it was my mind's way of telling me that I needed to slow down and take care of myself. Creating this session taught me about mutually beneficial relationships, as I learned more about myself, while also providing support and guidance to others.

I had started to experience nightmares and insomnia again, so I took time away after that session to refocus on my transformation. If you have ever had these concerns on your healing journey, you know that it can affect you in some strange ways as you try to create a new normal.

After my nightmares taught me more about what I needed to heal, I created my second Sharewell hosting session, titled "Empower-Her Voice: A Safe Space for Healing." This session was held for women only, so they could have a safe space to be able to share their concerns and fears, and to seek guidance when they were feeling stuck.

As I was able to support others who were (like me at one point) battling alone, I struggled to break my silence too. I understand how scary it is to step forward and state what has happened. It takes courage, bravery, and strength. The thing is, *you* have the same courage, bravery, and strength needed to share your own story. This is your invitation to do so.

The path that you take to share your story does not have to look like mine. I went from quietly journaling my story, to attending support groups, to creating my own healing sessions for others, and then into podcasting.

If you're interested in additional guidance, you can check out my podcast *Triumphant Over Trauma: Living Life Victoriously after Trauma*, which is available on all podcast listening platforms. This is what I mean by "you may start quietly, but once you start, it becomes easier to share in different ways."

Your path can begin at any time you choose, in any way that you feel comfortable. Keep in mind that you may feel nervous at first, and that is ok. Part of the healing journey is to learn to be comfortable when you are the most uncomfortable. Healing occurs out of your comfort zone, not inside of it.

You may also notice that once you start to share your story, others step up to support you in ways that you have never been supported before. Trauma has a way of connecting you more deeply to other people who want to see you happy, healthy, and free. I am one of those people for you.

You will start to notice that there are people who truly love you and will provide positive support with the best of intentions. This will make sharing your story so much easier as time moves forward.

When you choose to stay silent and avoid what has happened to you, this creates more bottled up emotions, leading to an increase in the pain that you are feeling. It is ok to be scared and fearful— the important thing is that you realize you matter, and that your story has power.

You may not notice it at first, but once you start to share your story openly, you begin to feel free, at peace, and safe. This takes some time, because when you first start to share, your thoughts may even be:

*What did I just do?*

*Did I share too much?*

*Will they still like me now that they know this part of me?*

All of these thoughts and the others that you may have are normal. Make sure that you allow yourself some time to sit with these thoughts and feelings so you can continue to process what has happened after you share your story.

It has been said that there is the part of your story that exists before the traumas occur and the part that exists afterwards, and the trauma sits between them.

Where you are now is the part where you are able to finally share your story, process what has happened, learn from it, and make small actionable steps to create the life that you have always dreamed of. This is the part where you feel loved, valued, heard, and seen. It's the part where you learn that you do not have to settle for anything less than you deserve.

## Actionable Step

Journal about a significant event in your life that has shaped you. Write it down or speak it aloud and record it without judgment, just as it is.

A note on journaling: journaling does not have to be pen or pencil to paper, it can be spoken in a voice note, or by using the video option on your phone. There are many ways to journal. Choose the way that you feel most comfortable with at first.

In time, you will be able to progress as your comfort level grows with sharing your story. I started with a pen and pencil on paper. I got to the point that I was writing so much that my hand started to cramp. When this happened, I moved to speaking into a voice note on my phone, and then progressing to video journaling.

Video journaling is a different beast at first as you actually see yourself (the camera is pointed at you) and you are able to view your nonverbal actions. In my experience, video journaling has been what has helped me to heal the most.

You are able to state how you feel openly, be one hundred with yourself, and also see when your actions (facial expressions, hand gestures, body movements) do not match with your words.

You are able to see yourself angry, smiling, laughing, and crying. You are able to see yourself as you exist in that moment. In order to get the most from the video journaling experience, this means that you must watch the video back to learn, gain clarity, and better understand what you are going through.

I still video journal especially when I am processing a situation and seeking to gain clarity. It is your choice how you want to complete this actionable step. Choose the right one for you.

If you are in therapy, you can also use your journaling to share with your therapist what you have been working through in between sessions. This may make it easier for you if you do not want to restate the situation.

If you want to share what you have written in a safe space, you can always email me at Gina@ginahamiltoncoaching.com. I will respond to you. Have fun with this activity, and remember that by sharing your story, you are showing strength and creating power.

# 3 | THE HEALING WITHIN: EMBRACING YOUR INNER WARRIOR

*"She believed she could, so she did."*

—R.S. Grey

There comes a moment when the silence becomes unbearable, when the voice within you refuses to be silenced any longer. It's a voice that has been stifled by pain, doubt, and fear, but it grows louder each day, demanding to be heard. For so long, you've kept it buried beneath the weight of your trauma, but now it pushes its way to the surface, urging you to help it break free.

The moment you shatter the silence, you begin to feel something you haven't felt in a long time—freedom. It's the first step toward embracing who you truly are, and more importantly, who you have yet to become.

Trauma may have changed you, reshaped the way you see the world, but the journey to healing, to reclaiming your power, will transform you in ways you never imagined.

This path is not an easy one. It requires grit, perseverance, and an unwavering belief that you can overcome any obstacle that life throws your way. Weakness does not define you. Instead, you are defined by having the strength to show up, day after day, with the courage to heal, to grow, and to pave a new path toward a brighter, more hopeful tomorrow.

Your inner warrior has always been there, waiting to rise, and now is the time to embrace that strength and let it guide you toward healing and wholeness.

The alarm blares to wake you up for another day. Figuring that just five more minutes will make all the difference, you hit snooze. You lie in bed, staring at the ceiling, and wonder if you have the strength to make it through the day.

You know that you need to get up and move, but the thought of calling in to work and doing nothing all day seems so enticing. Bed rot is certainly something that you are down with today, as last night was neither peaceful nor restful.

You dread putting on another fake smile, creating small talk, and helping to make sure that everyone else is ok (despite the fact that you are not). Doing all the small things to keep life going day to day has become so draining that you have zero interest or motivation in keeping this facade going.

You continue to lie there while the alarm goes off. Your five minutes are up, and you have a decision to make. Will you continue to lie there, or will you get up and start moving towards a brighter tomorrow?

You sigh heavily as you start to sit up on the side of the bed. You think of all the things that need to be done today and try so desperately to find the energy to get started.

You make it to the bathroom and look at yourself in the mirror. Only you are not seeing your reflection—you have not seen that in years. You are merely a shell of yourself trying to find your way back to who you think you are. *"Just who am I really, anyways?"* Even that is a question that has been deeply ingrained in your mind.

You wash your face, brush your teeth, get dressed, and make your way to the kitchen to try to eat. Self-care is certainly a large obstacle that looms over you every day. You struggle to take care of yourself because you have always taken care of others. While deeply compassionate of you, it has also prevented you from taking the best care of yourself.

You muster up the strength to grab your things and head out the door to work. Your day begins to unfold as you manage to silence your inner voice yet again. Time is running out …

The path that you took to get to this day is a path that you would never have wished on anyone. It's a path that has repeatedly torn you down into pieces of your former self.

While you have worked so hard behind the scenes to rebuild yourself, you are still struggling to break free from a past that has been painful, dark, and has introduced you to parts of yourself that you never would have met otherwise—the parts of you that you have felt were broken, fragmented, and hidden behind a fake smile (you know—the one you show to people to make them think you are ok).

You have learned how to lie to yourself and to run away from the emotions that cause you so much pain. You have gotten really good at distracting yourself with things that do not matter—scrolling on social media, engrossing yourself in petty gossip and drama, and binging this week's new favorite show. Your inner voice screams at you to listen to it, but you question if now is the time to set it free.

Part of the healing process is learning to truly listen to your inner guidance and realizing that you don't need external validation. When you begin to truly listen to yourself, believe in your abilities, and trust in your own journey, things begin to change in the most miraculous ways.

Had you not chosen to put yourself first and start your healing journey, these changes would have never been possible. This decision is certainly one that takes time, until you are caught off guard and forced to break your silence.

Once you make the decision to break your silence and start to embrace your healing journey, you also accept inner strength and resilience into your life. These two traits have been with you all along, though you were too busy fighting for survival to see them.

Each time you look at your fear and make the decision to address it with intention, you gain resilience and inner strength. Each time you finally speak up for yourself after being disrespected, countering every whispered "no" when you don't agree with what's being said to you, and every time you break contact with someone after they repeatedly cross your boundaries, you're setting boundaries to achieve the respect you deserve. This changes your inner world by showing yourself that you matter.

Think about it—even though it's overwhelmingly uncomfortable and nerve wracking when you choose to do things differently, with time, you also start to feel better, stronger, and more confident in your ability to handle adversity.

For those who have not faced trauma, inner strength and resilience are normally a foreign concept, because they are created by the least expected experiences in life. Accepting that you are able to live life on your own terms, and in the best way that you see fit, helps to drive your inner strength and resilience forward.

It's like going to school on the first day of the new school year. You may lie in bed for a while, you may hit snooze multiple times, and you may even be nervous to face all the unknowns before you arrive. However, you eventually make the choice to get out of bed, show up to school, and let the day unfold.

In this moment, with this choice, you have also begun to embrace your inner strength and resilience. Your healing journey is also asking you to step forward, just like it was your first day of school.

The path to embracing your inner warrior and starting your journey to heal within is different for everyone. You may find similarities with others, but your path is individualized for you and your continued growth. It is completely ok that it does not exactly match with someone else's path—it is not meant to. On this path, it is important to be kind, patient, loving, and gentle to yourself.

Depending on your traumas, you may also be reparenting yourself to heal the parts of you that were neglected during your upbringing. You are working to bridge the gaps between your inner child and who you are as an adult.

You will need to learn to give yourself the basic needs that you may not have been provided with—acceptance, love, nurturing, attention—as you move forward. This is another reason why self-care is so important.

Somewhere along the way, you may have been taught that it was of the utmost importance to take care of everyone else—which means putting yourself dead-last.

If you have not been able to take care of your needs, then how do you know what you require on a daily basis to survive and thrive? This is why it is so important for trauma survivors to come up with their own self-care plan.

If you are struggling with self-care, I have created the Radiant Mind & Soul Guide that will help you to create your own easily manageable self-care plan. You can get it here:

**bodyelementsmindelevation.com/
Radiant-Mind-and-Soul**

Accessing your inner strength and resilience can be as simple as creating a few moments each day to connect with yourself. During this time, you are able to see your fears, notice your emotions, and create small actionable steps to take as you move forward on your path.

When you take the time to connect with yourself, your inner strength and resilience grows. It is equally important that you are not shaming yourself for how you feel. You are allowed to feel how you feel.

Some days will feel awesome and other days not so much—more "meh" than anything. It's ok. Allowing yourself to feel will also help you heal. True inner balance comes from staying on the path.

By now, you have created a new path that you can see, or maybe you have just started on your healing journey and you are still searching for a path.

Embracing the unknown is scary, so you are working so hard to make sure that you know the outcome. But when you wait until you think you know the outcome, you end up not doing anything at all, and what you think will be the outcome may never even happen.

It is important during your healing journey that you become comfortable even in the most uncomfortable of moments, and embrace the unknown. There is no way that you will be able to predict every outcome before it happens.

If you sit and do nothing, fear will take over and make it harder for you to take that first step moving forward. You may not know everything that you need to know right now, and that is ok. Healing is a process that occurs over time, and you have the ability to make changes as you see fit.

You will have to start over multiple times in your healing journey, until you find the path that is meant for you. This is ok. Failure gives you the chance to expand your knowledge so you can make the best decisions as you continue to move forward.

## Actionable Step

Create a mantra, affirmation, or alter-ego that resonates with your inner warrior, and read it daily.

Sometimes creating an alter-ego helps us to heal. The alter-ego is created based on how we want to see ourselves, the characteristics and traits that we want to have, and how we want to feel as we work on our path to healing. You can even name your alter-ego.

Many people use alter-egos when they need to step into a version of themselves that is more courageous, empowered, and ready to take on the world at any given time (even if in this moment we would rather commit to bed rot).

If you are comfortable enough to do this, I invite you to create your alter-ego and see where she takes you. Visualizing your future self can also help you manifest that which you desire the most for your life.

Affirmations and mantras are meant to be positive. They are there to give you something to believe in even when you may not feel like believing in anything. They are there to lift you up when you are down and to help create a positive mindset while the negative is slowly flushed away.

Positive affirmations sound like this:

> "I am brave."
>
> "I have the courage to speak my truth and break my silence."
>
> "I love myself and who I am becoming."

You can use these, add to them, or create your own. Creation is part of the healing process. What will you choose to create today?

# 4 | THE STRENGTH IN VULNERABILITY: EMBRACING YOUR TRUE SELF

*"To share your weakness is to make yourself vulnerable; to make yourself vulnerable is to show your strength."*

—Criss Jami

Vulnerability can feel like a sudden jolt of fear—like someone jumping out of the shadows, catching you off guard, leaving you exposed and terrified. It's that heart-stopping moment when you want to retreat, to shut down, to pull the shades down and close yourself off from the world.

The terror of being seen—truly seen—can be overwhelming, tempting you to slip back into the silence that once kept your inner truth locked away. But in that very moment of fear, when you feel the urge to go dormant and hide, lies the potential for something incredible: the chance to let the light back in.

Vulnerability, though it may seem like weakness, is the bravest thing you can do. It's the act of standing in the darkness, opening the blinds, and allowing yourself to be known, flaws and all.

When you embrace vulnerability, you begin to meet your true self—the one who has been hidden beneath layers of pain, fear, and self-doubt. And though it may be scary, it's the light of vulnerability that sets you free, guiding you to a life of authenticity, where you can finally be who you were always meant to be.

As far back as you can recall, you have played it safe. You have kept yourself out of the limelight and prevented what you thought were any attention seeking behaviors. You have done this with the intent to keep yourself safe. While you have narrowly managed to complete this goal, you have also prevented yourself from learning who you truly are and realizing your full potential. Your existence has been kept completely private.

Think about it. The shame that you feel for the debilitating mishaps that have occurred in your life has kept you from sharing what you have really been battling behind closed doors and how you are truly feeling day to day.

Over the years, you have kept silent to protect the ones who would not protect you, wore winter clothes when it was summer to hide your battered body, and cut yourself so deeply at times so that you would be forced to feel because you have felt nothing.

You may have even narrowly avoided a car accident after another sleepless night caused you to fall asleep at the wheel. You have never shared this with anyone. You have battled for years alone, making sure to keep things on the DL, and to keep the peace for as long as you could.

However, lately nothing has been peaceful. You are struggling to get out of bed. Each day, you are stumbling like a toddler learning to walk. You want to cry when you fall, but there has been no one there to catch you and wipe your tears away.

You have felt like a failure in more ways than you can count, and still you do your best to show up. You have learned to hide your pain in silence, get up, wipe your tears away, and act like nothing has happened.

Now you are starting to question everything that you have done to this point, because it feels like things are not improving—they are only getting worse. Being vulnerable causes overwhelming fear in the heart of any survivor.

Avoidance has been one of the main cornerstones that you have utilized along your journey, so showing a side of yourself that you have fought to keep private can be deafening to your senses.

The thing is, as your traumatic experiences unfolded, how you responded then does not have to be how you will respond now. At this point, life is asking you to show up differently, and that requires you to do things that you have never done before. Hello, vulnerability!

When I first started to share what I was going through and maneuver the path of vulnerability, I was scared to death. I was so anxious and concerned over the potential outcomes that I remained silent for a really long time. Even though I had tried so hard to speak up before, I still did not feel heard, seen, or valued.

I thought, *Why risk being vulnerable and asking for help that I'm probably not going to receive?* I hated asking for help, and felt like if I wanted things done the right way, I had to do them all by myself. Then if I failed, there was only myself to blame. I was used to being blamed for everything that went wrong, so why not add something else to my plate? Who really cared, anyways?

Time passed and as I grew more comfortable in my skin, felt more steady on my feet, and created a path of healing—not only for myself but for others—I stepped up to the plate and tried vulnerability again. This time, I did it online, using social media platforms to share my story and connect with others who were battling alone like I was. I was scared to death, because I had family and friends who were following my pages. I had not spoken about what had happened to me, and no one was aware of the struggles that I was facing.

I drew from my inner strength and courage and created a small reel to share my story. This was one of the first reels that I had ever created. I would like to say that it was completed in a one and done fashion, but that was far from the truth.

It took me what felt like forever to open up and speak about it on camera—a video that I knew would be shared openly. Eek! Finally, I completed the reel and put it on social media, afraid and nervous about what I would hear.

The reel was posted on a Friday. I took the weekend to brace myself for what I worried would be massive negativity. When I opened my Instagram page (@blueeyedqtpi), I was met with positivity, the exact opposite of what I thought would happen.

Still extremely nervous, I moved on to my Facebook account (Gina Marie Hamilton). My fears had come true: a family member had verbally attacked me and my dad (who passed away in 2013—long before my vulnerable post).

I sat there in the bathtub staring at the phone screen, feeling pain, disbelief, and sadness. This was how I had felt around that side of the family for years, even before my parents divorced after 40 years of marriage. I tried to respond but soon realized that they had blocked me, which was the best outcome for me.

Being vulnerable changed me for the better. The things that I was once afraid of happening were occurring, but I was surviving them. A subtle smile came across my face. I had actually started to feel free again. No one will criticize you for sharing your story unless they have not done the work to accept their own story.

It takes courage, bravery, and trust to step forward and be vulnerable. After I took that first step, that did not mean that I could get on the nearest rooftop and scream everything that I had been through, but it helped me to open the shades and allow the light back in. After so much darkness, I was finally starting to feel something that I had not felt before—peace.

Turns out, in the days, months, and years that followed, I was able to finally let the light in all the way and embrace who I truly am. I continue to work on it daily by making small actionable goals that allow me to love who I am, be comfortable in my own skin, and live my life authentically.

Had I not taken those steps way back when to share my story, I probably would not be able to write this book today, or speak about healing from trauma and living life victoriously on my podcast. You have to feel comfortable enough to share your story and break the barriers that prevent you from being vulnerable.

Vulnerability does not have to be done perfectly. Oftentimes, it's imperfect action that helps us take our next steps forward. People will always have an opinion. How you choose to handle their opinions is up to you. You can't prove yourself to people who never listened to you in the first place. Save your energy and devote it to becoming the happiest, healthiest, and healed version of you.

When you live your life authentically, there is no more pretending, hiding, or shielding yourself from your truth. You can show up for yourself and be a woman who feels comfortable in her own skin (even on the days that you feel terrible).

Living authentically creates a sense of freedom that you have never experienced before. When it happens, the lightbulb will go off in your brain, and you'll say to yourself, "So this is what it feels like," as you smile and a sense of peace comes over you.

Being who you really are is essential to your healing process. When you continue to stay silent and conceal who you really are, your shadow self grows, as do the things that you will need to heal from. Your shadow self represents all the things that remain hidden that you choose not to deal with. More about that in the next chapter.

It is important for you to know that when you decide to be vulnerable and overcome what life has thrown at you, you are unlocking doors to opportunities that you never knew existed. You have survived one hundred percent of your worst days. You can survive being vulnerable too.

Vulnerability does not have to take place in one giant step. It can take place in small, manageable steps. It will feel odd at first, and you may have to be especially gentle with yourself—this is all ok.

Still struggling with self-care? Here's the link to my Radiant Mind & Soul guide, which will help you create a self-care routine that is easily manageable for you:

**bodyelementsmindelevation.com/
Radiant-Mind-and-Soul**

Making changes takes time and patience. This is part of the process. Once you take that first step to being vulnerable, you'll see the domino effect of all the new opportunities that open up based on this one decision.

Life is asking you to show up differently! So make the intentful decision and do it!

## Actionable Step

Identify one area of your life where you can allow yourself to be more vulnerable, and take a small step towards embracing it.

If you get stuck and want to share for additional guidance and support, feel free to email me so we can connect at gina@ginahamiltoncoaching.com. You've got this! On to the next part of your journey we go!

# 5 | SHEDDING THE PAST: RELEASING WHAT NO LONGER SERVES YOU

*"Release the past, capture the present, and embrace the future."*

—Billy Cox

Holding onto the past is like climbing a mountain with the heaviest backpack imaginable—each step forward feels like an impossible task, leaving you breathless, exhausted, and questioning whether you have the strength to reach the summit.

The weight of old wounds, regrets, and unresolved pain drags you down, making every movement sluggish and every breath labored. As you try to move forward, these burdens become chains that anchor you to a past that no longer serves you, but still has its hold on your heart.

But what if you could let it all go? What if, in one deliberately freeing act, you could unstrap that heavy load and feel the weightlessness of freedom?

Shedding the past is not just an act of release—it's a powerful declaration of your right to breathe with ease, to create inner peace, and to dispel the conflicts that have kept you from becoming who you were always meant to be.

In letting go, you don't lose anything—except the pain that has held you back. You gain the strength to move forward, unhindered and unburdened, toward the life you truly deserve.

You have fought the good fight by bottling up everything that you have dealt with to deal with it alone. In an effort to protect both others and yourself, you decided this was the best way to move forward.

Originally, you thought about reaching out for help or guidance, but you don't even know what that looks like in your life. When you thought about actually reaching out, you decided not to do so because you didn't want to be a burden to others.

Reaching out can also feel embarrassing, since you worry that you put yourself in the situation in the first place. However, when the problems started, they looked nothing like they do now. In the beginning, there was closeness, a sense of trust, and even love that you thought was unconditional.

As time moved forward, you realized there was only loneliness and despair, that trust was a thing of the past, and love—well, that's only given when you meet a series of impossible expectations.

You noticed that certain people felt that they should be able to control the way you spoke, behaved, and what you wore, so you stayed silent, on your best behavior, and asked for permission to wear anything. Your life was a bleak existence. However, this was months, or maybe years ago. Time has moved forward, and you are trapped somewhere in the past.

Insomnia wreaks havoc on your sleep, and nightmares repaint the things that you wish to escape. You're lucky if you're sleeping at all. Most nights you sleep so lightly that the drop of a pen would wake you up. Lack of rest causes you to struggle to keep it together when you are awake.

Before, it was always easy for you to keep it together—or at least, that's what you made people think. You showed up, looked the part, spoke the part, and became the part, but it was never you. It was a figment of your imagination that you created to shield yourself from the things happening in your life.

For example, I once received a passive-aggressive Christmas gift—a vacuum cleaner—from my then-husband as a statement that I needed to do more (beyond running the household and raising our twin sons). He presented it to me in front of his entire family, telling them that I had asked for it even though I never did.

I reacted meekly because, at that time, I was too afraid to speak my mind due to the repercussions that I would get when we got home, but the look on my face said otherwise. Privately, I felt angry, but I presented the quietest version of myself, smiled and nodded, and muttered a soft spoken "thank you."

There is no doubt that over the years people have made you believe things about yourself that were never true. You tried your best to ignore the lies, pretend like they did not hurt you, and go on living life like you never heard them. This is only one of many lies that you have tried to tell yourself so often that you thought you believed it—but not fully.

There are other times when the past has cut you so deeply that it was less painful to act as though it never existed. At least this way, what was forgotten will not be able to cause you any harm. Right? *Wrong.* This is utterly incorrect and will affect everything that you do moving forward.

If you continue to ignore the past, new relationships will become your previous relationships, as self-doubt, untrustworthiness, and jealousy start to cloud your vision, wreaking havoc on your mind. Your new bestie is wonderful until she starts getting closer with your significant other and ignoring you. Your new job has surpassed your desires, until the supervisor starts to degrade you. How did all this happen? Life was finally going good for a while.

The longer that you choose to carry the burdens of your past, the more likely they are to show up during your happiest moments. Then, everything starts to fall apart as you quickly rush to come up with solutions to put your life back together.

Overexplaining your actions, trying to prove who you are, seeking external validation, and making promises that you aren't sure you can keep. Ugh! What gives? You thought that everything you had done up to this point had created the happiness you were seeking.

Well, you're still climbing up the mountain with the heaviest backpack imaginable, equipped with only things that are holding you back and preventing you from reaching your goals. When will you realize that putting the backpack down and unpacking the things you don't need will allow you to move forward more easily, and with a new perspective on life?

Letting go of the past doesn't mean you have to forget everything that happened. It means letting go of the parts of the past that were painful, caused you to struggle, and created a pessimistic outlook on life.

It means holding onto the moments where you felt warmth in your heart and love in your soul, and exercising your innate ability to see life in a beautiful way. Clearing out and processing the pain that you have fought to hold onto for so long will help you to feel weightless and free.

When you allow yourself to release what no longer serves you, you are also creating a safe space within yourself that you can return to at any time. This safe space is something that you once had to fight for every time you did not feel safe, on the days that you felt unwanted and undesired, and when you were treated like an object and not like an individual with your own wants, needs, and thoughts.

It's the space that you so desperately desired when you just wanted to feel loved, admired, and respected. The truth is that this safe space has been there all along—you were just too busy trying to survive to see it.

The longer that you fight to hold on, the larger your shadow self becomes. Trapped inside your shadow self are all the things you buried because you did not want to deal with the fallout. The times where you felt unloved, unwanted, unappreciated, betrayed, embarrassed, and judged.

While you may think that locking up these feelings and throwing away the key is advantageous, it is not at all. In the darkest corners of your mind, these memories replay like a song on repeat, cranking up to the loudest volume possible when you are struggling. You know what the verses sound like?

> *"You're such a failure!"*
> *"Why do you even try? No one cares."*
> *"They'll never like you anyways."*

Holding onto things that you need to let go of will continuously affect your life until you make the decision to free yourself and let them go.

Taking the first step to meet all the versions of you that have experienced any kind of traumatic pain is hard. At times, it can be overwhelmingly difficult, and you may want to stop your healing journey altogether. When this happens, it is life that is asking you to dig deeper into your reserves of strength and resilience, and continue to show up.

When you keep showing up, your outlook on life will change, you will see with clarity, and the hardships of your past will be able to melt away like a lit candle. With any part of the healing journey, you need to have patience, gentleness, kindness, and love for yourself. This may even require you to use a word that you are not accustomed to using—the word "no."

Healing is a multifaceted journey that will require you to show up in ways that you may have never imagined. When life requires you to show up differently, you might even question yourself and think, *"There's no way I can do that."*

With the trust and belief in yourself that you have started to create by doing the tough things, you know that there is a way that you can do it. You just have to find the way that is right for you.

Remember, this is *your* healing journey. It does not have to look like everyone else's. If you try something and you do not like the outcome, you'll learn a new solution to try if the past repeats itself. Most likely it will, until you have learned to cope with what has happened to you.

## Actionable Step

Write down things from your past that you are ready to release. Consider performing a small ritual, like tearing up the paper, as a symbolic act of letting go.

Please remember to be kind to yourself during this actionable step. It will require you to become comfortable enough while being in an uncomfortable part of the transition.

You may also notice that your mind starts to lock up or you have the feeling that your brain has packed itself up and walked off. This is all normal—you are working on confronting things that you have only alluded to for so long.

If you need to, set the activity aside for a brief period of time and return to it when you are able. Remember to practice self-care after this activity and to be kind, gentle, patient, and loving to yourself. It does get better.

# 6 | THE POWER OF "NO": SETTING BOUNDARIES WITH LOVE

*"The oldest, shortest words—'yes' and 'no'—are those which require the most thought."*

—Pythagoras

Are you tired of saying "yes" when your heart is screaming "no"? Of constantly giving away pieces of yourself until you feel depleted, exhausted, and invisible in your own life? Each time you say "yes" when you really mean "no," is like keeping your foot on the gas pedal, speeding through life with no time to slow down or breathe.

You've become an expert at showing up for everyone else, but somewhere along the way, you've forgotten how to show up for yourself. But here's the truth: saying "no" is not selfish—it's an act of self-love. It's the pause, the break, the much-needed breath that allows you to care for yourself in ways that replenish your soul.

"No" gives you space to nourish your mind, body, and spirit so that you can show up fully, not only for others, but also for yourself. It's not a betrayal of those you love—it's a gift to them, allowing them the opportunity to step up and handle things on their own.

The responsibility of meeting everyone's needs is not yours to carry alone. In saying "no," you reclaim your power, set boundaries with love, and finally begin to honor and care for yourself in the ways you so deeply deserve.

You have kept your foot on the gas pedal for years, traveling to an unknown destination. Things pass you by in a blur as you're going 100 mph on what feels like a never-ending interstate. You question when it will end so that you can take a break.

You've been exhausted, depleted, and out of motivation for a while now. Despite this, you continue to push yourself forward until out of nowhere, a roadblock appears and you have no choice but to hit the brake so hard that it gives you whiplash.

You have just hit burnout. You're completely exhausted, and you have no ability to move forward. You're trapped in an unknown location.

You realize that your trusted backpack, which you recently emptied of all the things that no longer serve you, is in the vehicle with you. You reach for your backpack, hopeful that it will provide you with the tools to move forward, but you realize that you haven't prepared for this situation.

On this journey, you have repeatedly said "yes" to others when you really meant "no." You have continuously depleted yourself by giving to others when you had nothing left to give.

You feared that if you couldn't provide for others, they would decide they didn't need you around anymore. Your innate fear of abandonment is real, but what if they chose to stay? What if people want to be around you not because of what you can provide, but because of who you are as a person?

You believe that if you do not give everything of yourself to the people around you, they will no longer need you, and you will end up alone. You're so afraid of abandonment that you're burning yourself out to avoid it, but you can't drive at 100 mph forever. By forcing you to come to a screeching halt, life is showing you that if you want to survive, you need to do things differently.

While you worry that saying "no" would be the death of you, it will not. It is actually the beginning of a new you. The version of you that seeks to make your own needs a priority is the healthiest version of you that is possible.

The question is, are you willing to make the necessary changes to avoid burnout and continue to be there for yourself and others you love so deeply? If so, you will have to embrace the practice of setting loving boundaries (which includes saying "no" at times).

To any trauma survivor, creating and setting boundaries can be a downright scary experience. It can cause panic, emotional discord, and fear throughout your heart, so that you just want to sit down, say "no way!", and shut down in order to avoid it.

However, I can assure you that when you start small by setting just one boundary, that single act of self-respect will create a ripple effect, gradually empowering you to set more boundaries and reclaim your time, energy, and peace without guilt or hesitation. This will require time and patience on your part.

When you first start to create and put boundaries into place, it will feel weird, uncomfortable, and overwhelming. Your mind will start to play tricks on you and make you question and doubt yourself.

This is another reason to let go of the things that no longer serve you, because letting go makes it easier to move past your scary thoughts. When that happens, you will know that you are on the right path, doing what is best for you. Embracing these emotions and allowing yourself to feel them will also help you to move forward, one small step at a time.

The first step in creating boundaries is to set aside some time to think about your needs and create small actionable steps to make sure they are met. Maybe you want some downtime at night, but lately, everyone wants to connect with you just as you're winding down for the evening. You could try setting aside a specific time for people to contact you, or turn notifications off on your phone a few hours before bed.

Of course, you could also tell anyone that normally contacts you during those hours that you are taking time to yourself, and you will not respond during that time frame. This small step will prepare them for when you put your plan into action. It will also help ease you into this decision, so you have time to get used to it as you work towards creating time for yourself.

Maybe the mornings are the most hectic and chaotic for you, and you would like to make time for a slower morning to start your day. This may require you to get up a little earlier than you usually would, but it would allow you to enjoy your coffee in silence or even take five minutes to stretch to help wake you up.

This would be a small, actionable step toward achieving a self-care goal. To reduce pressure on yourself, remember that you do not even need to tell anyone you are going to get up earlier.

There are all sorts of things that you can try in an effort to set boundaries and create a life that runs smoothly and peacefully. Saying "no" may not be something you're used to, though.

I'm sure if you took five minutes to think about all the things that you wish you would have said "no" to, you would be able to come up with something—even a small list. Moving forward, you could look back at that list when you aren't sure if you really want to say "yes," or if you just feel pressured to say "yes" out of guilt.

The first time that you say "no," it may even come out as a whisper, and people may be surprised. They may even ask again, to see if you are sure. You do not have to provide a reason for saying "no." It is a complete sentence on its own.

Once you say "no" the first time, it becomes so much easier to say it when you truly feel that way and need some time for yourself. Do not miss out on this opportunity to meet your needs and practice self-care.

Speaking of self-care, how is that going for you now that you are further into your journey? Still struggling at times? That is ok. It can take some time to create a routine that you can follow consistently.

It's also ok for you to remove things that are no longer serving you, and try new things in your daily self-care routine. This is how you will find out what helps you to feel refreshed, at peace, and joyful and fulfilled.

If you're still struggling, please feel free to check out my Radiant Mind & Soul Guide. It can be found here:

**bodyelementsmindelevation.com/
Radiant-Mind-and-Soul**

Saying "no" is not only a part of self-care, but it is also a part of self-love. Self-love is another necessity that you may struggle to provide for yourself. This is also ok.

When you have had to fight for so long to be accepted, wanted, and valued by others, it is hard to understand why you should be the one to provide these things to yourself.

Sometimes during the healing process, you will have to unlearn previous mind conditioning to learn new, healthier thought patterns and behaviors that align with your true self, allowing you to grow and thrive. Being able to truly love and accept yourself will make your healing journey that much easier to navigate as you continue to move forward.

We have just barely scratched the surface when it comes to creating and setting boundaries. However, as with any skill, it is important to take things slow and be patient with yourself as you learn to set boundaries.

You do not have to be in any sort of a rush or apply pressure on yourself. Just start with taking some time to reconnect with yourself and learn more about the needs that you need to fulfill.

To get started, here are some examples of needs waiting to be met:

- improving your self-worth
- finding meaningful, trustworthy connections
- building a support network for when you need it the most
- empowering yourself to take control of your life
- reminding yourself that you are worthy of a good life
- and realizing that you are enough, even if you have never felt that way before.

This is not an exhaustive list—just one to get you started in case you are stuck and having trouble.

## Actionable Step

Identify one boundary that you need to set in your life. Figure out how you will communicate this boundary to others, and write it down.

Starting with just one boundary and finding small actionable steps that you can take to put it in place will make it easier to enforce the other boundaries that you need to set. Begin with the one that would be the easiest to start with, and devise your plan to set it.

You can do this! You have accomplished so much with your determination and motivation to heal, so there is no doubt in my mind that you'll be able to complete this step as bravely and courageously as you have the other actionable steps.

# 7 | BOUNDARIES AS BRIDGES: BUILDING SAFE SPACES FOR HEALING

*"The darkest night is often the bridge to the brightest tomorrow."*

—Jonathan Lockwood Huie

Creating boundaries is not about building walls to shut people out, but about building bridges that lead to a stronger, healthier, and more fulfilled version of yourself. Boundaries are the gateway to deep, meaningful connections—with others, yes, but most importantly, with yourself.

After trauma, the world can feel like an unsafe place, and you may constantly find yourself questioning your surroundings, wondering if you're truly protected. But here's the truth: safety begins from within. Until you've created a safe space inside your own mind and heart, the external world will always feel uncertain.

Boundaries are the tools that help you carve out that internal sanctuary, giving you the confidence and peace of mind to step into the world without fear. They allow you to honor your needs, protect your energy, and walk through life knowing that no matter what changes or challenges come your way, you have the strength and skillset to navigate them with grace.

Boundaries are not barriers; they are bridges to the life of safety, confidence, and fulfillment that you deserve.

It was a couple of years ago, but I can remember it like it was yesterday. I had just pulled up to a new pharmacy to refill a prescription. I checked to make sure that I was at the right location before getting out of the car and walking inside.

I was in a good mood—it was a beautiful day, and after this small errand, I was headed to the gym for a lift. As I pulled the door open, the handle felt cold to the touch. I took one step inside and my world completely changed. Suddenly, without warning, I became so afraid that I wanted to turn around and walk right out the door, but I still needed my prescription.

It is so blindsiding how trauma can affect you. Just when you think you are fine, suddenly something happens and you are not. I remember thinking, *"What just happened? I was fine before walking in here."*

The rest of my interactions inside the pharmacy felt just as bad as my first step inside. There was so much clutter on the ground that you could barely walk anywhere, and I questioned how they were still able to operate with such a clear safety hazard.

I looked closer at the things that were hanging on the walls and behind the counter—dolls, tons of them, creepily staring at me. I flashed back to my grandmother's house as a kid and saw the very same thing—tons of dolls staring at me. I never felt safe there, and the reminder prevented me from feeling safe in the pharmacy.

My interaction with the staff felt cold and judgemental, like how I was treated after my parents got a divorce. I breathed in short, choppy breaths that I knew were not efficiently oxygenating me. Finally, I had my prescription in hand and I walked out the door.

Once I was outside, I breathed a very loud sigh of relief, much like you would if you were frustrated. I wasn't frustrated—my system was rebooting itself after leaving the chaotic environment that had triggered a painful childhood memory.

Stuck between my past and the current moment, I had to repeatedly remind myself that I was safe. It was only after I arrived at the gym parking lot that I started to breathe slightly easier.

I immediately grabbed my phone and started to video journal, not realizing that I was in a true panic attack, which had launched an asthma attack on top of everything else. I caught everything on tape.

Later, I would watch my journal entry and realize how I felt as a kid, process my bottled up emotions, and see how I looked when I was experiencing a panic attack and an asthma attack at the same time.

This is when I would start to learn more about my flashbacks, what I needed to do when I had them, and the strange thing that my brain did when I did not feel safe (brain fog and numbness as my brain packed up and left—aka dissociation). I had just watched myself have a full meltdown on screen. All of this occurred before I started instituting boundaries.

They say that there is life before a certain point and after. Before I created boundaries, my protective walls were so high that no one was able to reach the top, and I always feared for my safety.

This usually led to me arriving everywhere about 30 minutes early, so I had time to have a panic or anxiety attack beforehand. I had to spend so much time repeatedly reminding myself that "I'm ok," and completing breathing exercises so that I wouldn't hyperventilate so much that I became dizzy. At some point, I realized all of this had to stop.

I just wanted to be at peace, feel safe, and know that I could handle anything thrown my way, but that felt so far away. I started reading more about dissociation, and learned that it is a mechanism triggered by your brain to protect you when you are feeling overwhelmed and unsafe.

This realization triggered a bunch of changes for the positive. It also showed me that if I could come up with some sort of a plan, I could truly feel safe—for the first time in my life.

After this, my flashbacks and dissociation kicked into high gear, and I realized how important my self-care routine was. When my flashbacks and dissociation were that intense, it was because I felt unsafe.

When I took the time to ask myself *"What triggered me?"* I could trace that trigger to its origin. Then, I could provide myself what I needed in order to dismantle the trigger so it would no longer be an issue.

My self-care routine started to emerge, and on the days that I felt terrible (some refer to them as "mental health days"), I ramped up my self-care routine even more.

Turns out that taking the time to listen to what I needed and provide it for myself, also helped me feel safe internally. As I continued to care for myself, I started to really believe I was safe, and my flashbacks and dissociation, along with my panic attacks, became less intense and frequent.

The path to creating boundaries will not be the same for everyone. Even though I was terrified, going to the pharmacy that day was an eye opening experience for me. Had it not happened, I don't honestly know when I would have taken the time to set boundaries in my life. It was certainly not an overnight process.

It took time to determine what I needed the most, so I could learn how to use the skills I already had to meet my needs. Once I determined what required my attention, I then had to figure out how to provide it to myself. That definitely took some work—I was so used to taking care of everyone else that I did not know how to take care of myself. I could tell you what everyone else needed before I could tell anyone what I needed.

I decided to take a whole new path that I had never traveled before: make myself the priority. This meant after my last relationship ended in 2020, I chose myself and fully committed to my healing journey (including finding out who I really was outside of what others wanted). This was when I would learn more about boundaries and which ones were the best ones for me to create.

You may experience something similar to what I did at the pharmacy, or you may have a different experience altogether. Maybe you are tired of repeated patterns, and wish they would stop. Or you are feeling stagnant in your relationships, desiring a deeper and more meaningful connection than the shallow ones that you have had previously.

Creating boundaries and implementing them into your daily life will help you get there—they will also help you to develop a deeper connection with yourself along the way. After all, unless you have learned those details for yourself, you cannot tell someone what you need and how you need to be loved.

Remember, to start creating boundaries, you have to take some time to determine what you need. Once you understand your needs, then you are able to devise small actionable ways to meet those needs. Choose something small to start with, and begin implementing the boundary.

If you try it and it does not work, that is completely ok. Do not beat yourself up. Instead take some time and state what you tried and why it did not work. This is not an overnight process, so it might take some time to determine if it worked.

It will be uncomfortable at first, but with time and patience, it will gradually become easier. You can do this. Just think about how much better you will feel and use that as your internal motivation to continue pushing yourself forward.

If you are feeling overwhelmed, then allow yourself to take a break so you can recharge and feel better. You are learning a new skill that will help you navigate change, so be patient, kind, loving, and gentle with yourself through this part of your healing journey.

Boundaries do not come in a one size fits all design. Each individual needs to create their own boundaries based on what they need, and what helps them to survive and thrive abundantly. They can always be adjusted, scrapped, or added to.

Do not be afraid to start saying "no" more often, to place your self-care needs above other people's wishes, and if needed, to let go of the toxic people and places in your life. For example: the pharmacy that I talked about in the beginning is a place that I no longer visit.

Keep in mind that your boundaries will most likely change as your hard work and dedication helps you grow and improve.

## Actionable Step

Create a list of personal boundaries that will support your healing process. Reflect on how these boundaries will help you build a safer, healthier environment.

This list does not have to be perfect. It does not even have to be in complete sentences—it can be in fragmented form. Keep the list close to you, so you can add to it at any time. This is just a starting point, and by no means does it need to be concrete.

Some of the boundaries that you create may stick with you for the rest of your life, and you may toss some, never to be used again. Your boundaries will probably change as you move forward on your healing journey—this is normal, as it shows that you are changing and adapting as you grow.

# 8 | SACRED SELF-CARE: NURTURING YOUR MIND, BODY, AND SOUL

*"Nurturing yourself is not selfish—it's essential to your survival and your well-being."*

—Renee Peterson Trudeau

Self-care is not a luxury—it's a lifeline. In the aftermath of trauma, when the world feels heavy and fragmented, the simple act of caring for your mind, body, and soul can feel like the only thread keeping you together. Yet, this daily practice is so much more than just survival—it's a gateway to reclaiming your power.

Self-care allows you to reconnect with yourself in the present moment, offering you the space to breathe, reflect, and dive deeper into your own self-discovery and transformation. It's a deliberate act of love, a necessary ritual that strengthens you from the inside out, providing the clarity, peace, and focus to keep moving forward even when life feels like it could unravel at any moment.

On the healing journey, self-care is essential—it grounds you when your emotions spiral, it brings clarity when everything feels chaotic, and it helps you to take small, actionable steps toward the life you were always meant to live. Through these sacred moments of care, you don't just survive—you thrive, turning your pain into power and nurturing your soul back to wholeness.

*"I am so tired of feeling this way! I have had enough!"* How many times have you caught yourself saying this? You end up feeling so exhausted that it takes days to put yourself back together again, and you still feel like you can barely function.

In this period of time, you have zero patience, a short fuse, and no mental space to do anything. You're just done with it all. *Done.* If one more thing is asked of you, the already heavy plate that you are carrying will break and shatter into a million pieces! Ugh! *"How did I even get to this point … again? I thought I had it all figured out."*

After you have taken the time to put yourself back together, everything hits you all at once. Suddenly, you are overwhelmed all over again. Now the question is, *"Why did I stop in the first place? I should have just kept on going."* You did what was right for you in the moment.

Life provided you with a staunch reminder that before you could take care of anything else, you needed to sit down and take care of yourself. But now, the dishes, laundry, bills, kids' schedules, work meetings, and all the rest of it feel like a ton of bricks that you are carrying on your shoulders. If you do not use this opportunity to create a plan and change the way that you are living, within time, you'll burn out again. Just what is it that you are lacking, anyways?

You have repeatedly overlooked one thing on your healing journey—a daily self-care plan that helps to meet your needs, provides space and time to breathe, and allows you some downtime to reconnect with yourself.

In any healing journey, self-care is a pivotal step to help you move forward. During the periods of darkness that erode your mind and make you feel paralyzed, it is this step in the healing journey that helps to keep you safe and reminds you that you can do anything that you set your mind to. It is the crawl before the walk and the walk before the run.

When you are so dissociated that you can't even remember what happened if someone asked you (unless you remembered to write it down), it is self-care that gives you the ability to bring yourself back to the present.

While self-care routines look different for everyone, they are still essential. The steps in your self-care routine may also change as you move deeper into your journey of self-discovery and transformation. This is ok. The healing journey is an ever-changing, fluid movement, and you are allowed to do parts of your life over until you feel good about them.

When you finally feel as though you got it right, you will feel a different sort of peace come over you, and you will know that you have what it takes to conquer anything you put your mind to. The best way to meet your needs on a daily basis is to form a self-care plan to take care of your mind, body, and soul. You do not have to wait for someone else to meet your needs—you can meet them all by yourself.

For instance, you just got off from an exhausting day at work. You've been busy meeting deadlines for reports, taking on extra work to help fulfill a company goal, and you've had very little time to even get something to eat and drink, or go to the bathroom. You feel like you are hitting burnout again—even though you've been working so hard to come out of it.

When you pick the kids up, they're so excited to tell you about their field trip, which you could not attend due to work constraints. *Sigh.* This is something else that weighs on your mind—not being able to attend their field trips, and missing out on time with them since they are not always in your care (hello, shared custody!).

You know they are excited and you do not want to be the Debbie Downer, but you have a headache, they are talking too loudly, and you have desperately needed a few moments of peace and quiet all day. As the light turns red, you rest your head on your hands, and suddenly you speak up—quietly and politely.

You ask the kids if they can just give you five minutes of peace and quiet, so you can truly be present to hear the joys of their day. They realize that you have had a very bad day, and provide the silence that you need for those five minutes.

You have just met the need that has required your attention all day. Go you! Five minutes pass, and you ask your kids to tell you about their day. They express their excitement and tell you in great detail about their field trip.

You are back on track and ready to be present and tackle life once again.

If you practice self-care daily instead of waiting to burn yourself out, you will not have to take a full day, or even several days in a row, to rest. Five minutes here and there, or longer when you need it the most, can help you to stay on track, clear your mind, and keep you connected and grounded. It can be five minutes in silence, journaling your feelings, listening to music, or even sitting outside in nature.

Taking the time that you need for yourself every day leads to a happy, healthy, and whole version of yourself. You will continue to face periods of burnout until you have learned to create a self-care routine that you can practice daily and with ease.

Still having trouble with creating a self-care plan? Or do you feel like your plan needs some revising? If so, I got you. The Radiant Mind & Soul Guide will provide what you need to get started, and help revise any self-care plan that you have already created. You can get it here:

### bodyelementsmindelevation.com/ Radiant-Mind-and-Soul

Any part of the healing journey, especially change, requires patience and time. This may be a brand new skill that you are learning—if so, that's ok.

Make sure that when you are creating your self-care plan, you are covering all the elements of you: your mind, body, and soul. It may even help to write down a list of things that would fulfill each of those needs.

An example might look like this:

> **Mind** (state the need, then a workable solution)
> 1. Some peace and quiet—scheduling five minutes throughout the day.

2. Learning something new—reading five pages of a book before you go to sleep.
3. Ridding yourself of negativity and toxicity—scheduling time for digital detox.

**Body** (state the need, then a workable solution)
1. Wanting to feel better about yourself—finding a workout to feel healthier and release endorphins that help you feel good.
2. Connect with how you are feeling—taking time to journal and release bottled emotions.
3. To have more energy—looking at what you are eating and drinking make sure it is providing the nourishment you require.

**Soul** (state the need then a workable solution)
1. Wanting to express yourself creatively—learn a new artistic hobby (think painting, coloring, drawing).
2. Deeper connections—reach out and talk to a trusted friend.
3. Wanting to be more mindful and present—start a gratitude journal.

This is just an example. Your self-care plan does not have to look like this at all. Some of the things listed above may be of interest to you—if so, feel free to add them to your self-care routine and see if you like how they make you feel.

Self-care routines are supposed to add joy, fulfillment, and peace to your day. If you realize that a step on your self-care plan is not helping you feel better, you may want to look at other solutions for that area of your life.

Keep in mind that since you are not accustomed to practicing self-care, it may feel odd and strange at first. Please allow yourself some time to adjust to the change.

## Actionable Step

Design a simple self-care routine that includes one activity each for your mind, body, and soul. Commit to practicing it daily.

Now is your chance to create a self-care plan that works well for you, keeping in mind that you can change it at any time. You may want to start with one thing and get used to doing that, then add in more steps accordingly. It's best to try to anchor it with something else you are already doing, as this makes the new addition easier to complete.

As an example, you could choose to read a book before bed. Carry out your usual night time routine (wash your face, brush and floss your teeth, go to the bathroom, wash your hands), then grab your book, find a comfortable place, and start to read.

This is what I mean by anchoring the new self-care step to ones that you are already doing. This will make it easier for you to find the time to practice self-care daily.

# 9 | THE PATH TO PEACE: FORGIVING YOURSELF AND OTHERS

> *"Forgiveness is the gift of releasing yourself from the past and unclogging your barrier to joy."*
>
> —Amara Honeck

Inside, it feels like you're beating against the walls of a cage, desperate to escape. Every day, the same memories replay over and over in your mind, like a broken record stuck on the part of the song you hate the most.

The pain is so intense, so overwhelming, that it silences you—stealing your voice, your energy, and your will to face the world. You've shut down, again and again, unable to find a way to release the storm of anger and hurt that rages inside.

The betrayal by those who were supposed to love you the most has left you with a short fuse, and when it flares, you find yourself pushing everyone away, including yourself.

You've become a stranger in your own skin, trapped in a cycle of pain and resentment, wondering if you'll ever find peace. But here's the truth—there is a way out.

Forgiveness is not about excusing the ones who hurt you, but about setting yourself free. It's the path to reclaiming your peace, releasing the weight of your past, and opening the door to healing.

By this time, you have become so accustomed to your internal rage that when it hits, you have learned to just ignore it. You know that if you try to fight it, you will just end up hurt and exhausted.

Sometimes, when the rage is so strong, you have even thought about hurting the ones who have harmed you the most … just like they harmed you. You try your best not to let these intrusive thoughts fill your mind, but when the rage hits, there is nothing that you can do to stop it.

Your mind is stuck on the song that you hate the most and continues to play repeatedly, making you want to scream and throw your hands up, even though you would never behave this way in reality unless someone was nose-to-nose screaming in your face.

You decide to try to play music that will hopefully change the song playing in your head, but you struggle to find something that will replace it. The song is getting louder and louder to the point that you can no longer take it. What will it take to clear the red that you see during a fit of rage?

The path to clear the reddened rage is one that you have not traveled before—at least not completely. To free yourself from the gross disrespect and mistreatment of others, you have to walk down the path of forgiveness.

You start to realize that a person can only treat you in the same way that they treat themselves. You see that they are projecting the way they look at themselves onto you.

As much as you tried to do everything for them and love them more than they hate themselves, this would have never changed them. They have to be willing to make the changes they need for themselves by going on their own healing journey and turning their own pain into power.

When you start to see that people can only meet you where they have met themselves, you will start to feel free. You'll also realize that if you are both at different phases of life, you will probably feel mismatched.

You will probably wonder, *"Are they the people I want to be around?"* When you start to question yourself in this manner, that should prompt you to look deeper into this thought. Until you take the time to address this thought, it will continue to play in your mind—similar to your reddened rage.

Just because you may be in different phases of life does not mean that something is wrong with you—or with them. It just means that the things you try in order to rectify the situation may not get through to them—and you do not have to keep trying if they aren't listening.

You know that you did everything you could to keep the relationship flourishing. You provided love when it was not given to you, you showed up ready to help when you did not receive the same support, and you actively listened even when you felt ignored. These are the mismatches that I am talking about.

You are giving so much when you receive so little in return because you are a kind-hearted, deeply loving woman with a heart of gold. You want to be there 100 percent for those that you deeply care for, even at your own expense. However, life is now providing you with a change of perspective, by asking you to show up for yourself as well.

The perspective shift you need in order to cross the bridge to joy and wholeness has to do with forgiveness. When you were younger, you were probably told, "Be the bigger person and forgive them," or "You'll feel better if you say you are sorry." So you apologized when others wanted you to, and you did not feel any better—not even in the slightest.

Instead, you resented the ones who wanted you to apologize, and the people you apologized to. Each time you apologized when you did nothing wrong, you felt silenced, and that the mistreatment you received from the other person was seen as justified. Due to this, forgiveness has been the furthest thing from your mind during your healing journey.

Being able to open your mind to forgiveness also opens your heart. With this type of forgiveness, it is not necessary to contact the person and say, "I forgive you," unless you want to do so.

Instead, you can forgive the other person for their actions, as well as yourself for the ways that you may have negatively responded. You can see that they are responsible for their actions and you are responsible for yours.

Sometimes, moving on means that you do so without ever receiving an apology. This is also ok. If you choose to wait for an apology that you may never receive, you may never be able to move on. This choice is on you.

Despite what anyone else may tell you, your decisions are important. Every choice you make in life will affect the next one, and the one after that. When you start to notice that your circumstances are not changing, and you feel like you are going in circles, this is your opportunity to make changes in your life that will break the cycle of repetition.

The question is, "What needs to be done differently to move past the stagnant areas of my life?" This answer is dependent on the individual.

When you choose forgiveness, it enables you to see where they are in their life and where you are on your own. It opens your eyes to a different perspective, so you can see what has happened with more clarity.

When you are able to change the way you look at things, you deepen your self-discovery and personal transformation. You learn why you did what you did, why you said the hurtful things you said, and why you behaved in a way that was totally out of character. It takes courage to realize that you could have handled certain situations better.

Forgiveness provides the vehicle for perspective shifts, growth, and changes in your behavior. By learning from the traumatic situations you experienced, you can change the way that you live your life moving forward.

Forgiveness does *not* mean that you excuse the behavior, but that you learn and adapt from it so you can continue on your path. Embracing forgiveness will take time and patience, but you will eventually begin to notice that your rage has diminished and the record that was once stuck in the same place has finally stopped.

Your mind will become clearer and free from the constraints of your past. You will begin to look at life differently and realize that you can make changes at any time on your journey, which will provide you with liberation, freedom, and empowerment.

## Actionable Step

Write a letter of forgiveness, whether to yourself or someone else. You don't need to send it; the act of writing is the healing step.

Writing a letter to someone—including yourself—can be a difficult step to take. As always, be patient and kind with yourself on this step. If you want to send the letter, it is ok to do so. Do what feels right in your heart.

# 10 | EMPATHY AS A SUPERPOWER: HEALING THROUGH COMPASSION

> *"When you start to develop your powers of empathy and imagination, the whole world opens up to you."*
>
> —Susan Sarandon

Empathy is not just a feeling; it's a bridge, a connection to the soul of another. It allows you to sit with someone in their pain, even when you don't fully understand it, and to hold space for their emotions without judgment.

When you meet someone exactly where they are, you are not only witnessing their truth—you're also deepening your understanding of your own. Empathy teaches us that every story, every wound, is unique. By opening our hearts to others, we learn to open our hearts to ourselves.

Imagine sitting with a friend who has endured their own trauma, feeling the heaviness in their voice, the weight of their silence. You're not there to fix it, but to simply be there for them.

Empathy isn't just an act of kindness—it's a superpower that heals and transforms. By embracing empathy, you aren't just helping others heal; you're allowing yourself to break through the barriers that have kept you from fully embracing your own healing journey.

There will be times when you won't know how to respond to the situations life presents. You will have to dig deep to meet someone on a level you've never reached before. Even when you don't know how to navigate the moment, choosing to sit with someone in their pain and give them a space for self-expression can touch them profoundly—and may even change you.

When you choose empathy, you're not trying to fix, solve, or take care of anything. Instead, you are choosing to show up differently, to truly sit with another person in their pain. As you listen to them and feel their emotions, you may start to recognize parts of their story that mirror your own. This recognition allows you to view your own story in a way you never have before.

By being there for someone else, you are also being there for yourself. When you notice the parallels between your stories, you have an opportunity to provide comfort—not by solving anything, but by showing the other person they are not alone and giving them the space to release their emotions without fear of judgment.

It provides time and space for the person who is stating their pain to be able to connect with the areas of their life that they are struggling with the most—an opportunity that may not have happened otherwise. In our busy lives, doing life, we rarely take time to just be and connect with ourselves on a deeper level. When someone takes time and creates space to truly share how they are feeling, the mask of "I'm fine" (when they are really not) falls off.

I remember taking a telehealth call from an older patient whose health was deteriorating. He wanted to discuss contacting his physician for an injection that would knowingly end his life. While I had never faced this situation before in my own life, he felt comfortable enough with me to share how he was feeling as he knew that his life would no longer improve. The conversation made me a bit uncomfortable because this was a thought process that I had never entertained in my own mind. However, I held space for him and actively listened while he shared his thoughts and deepest innermost feelings.

It was while listening to him that I also realized that parts of his story matched mine. I learned more about who he was the closest to and deemed the most important in his life—his son. At one point this was me in the lives of my parents—who have now passed. I learned more about how he felt to leave his child and how leaving him was causing an internal struggle of feeling shameful and awful. I questioned if this was how my parents felt when they left me in their death. Suddenly, I started to see things differently and learned from another perspective. Had this moment not happened, no matter how uncomfortable it was at first, I would not have been able to hold space for someone else in their pain and further connect with myself on a deeper level. The rate of my healing seemed to have sped up.

Choosing an empathetic perspective has the power to change your life. It provides a strong and sturdy bridge over unhealed wounds that can feel like a raging river, and on the other side is the opportunity to help others–including yourself.

In this space, your unhealed wound is no longer oozing and in need of attention and can finally start to close. It will no longer cause you noticeable pain. In the most unlikely of circumstances, you've just received the answers you have been waiting for in order to heal the wound.

Because you have shown great consistency, gentleness, and patience with yourself and others on your healing journey, life has brought you this opportunity to heal on a deeper level.

Making the deliberate choice to overcome your trauma and turn your pain into power is certainly overwhelming at times. By embracing discomfort, choosing to stop avoiding your pain and allowing yourself to feel it to its fullest extent, and deciding to do things differently than you normally would, you are going on a journey that will change you for the better.

You will notice massive shifts in your thoughts, in the way you carry yourself, in how you treat people when they are being disrespectful to you, and in your ability to hold space for others to share their own pain.

Had you not chosen this journey, these changes would probably not have happened until you chose to stop ignoring them and putting them off for another day.

Not too long ago, you chose to take the heavy backpack off your shoulders and empty it of the things that no longer served you. When you made this decision, you said goodbye to anger, resentment, rage, shame, low self-worth, lack of confidence, and anything else weighing you down from your past.

After you emptied it, you refilled it with the tools that you have picked up during your healing journey—things like increased self-awareness, improved confidence, internal peace, enhanced self-worth, boosted safety and stability, emotional regulation, and the newest tool added to your skillset: empathy.

This path has not always been easy for you, but by choosing to show up differently for yourself, you have also given yourself the power to help others on their own healing journeys.

## Actionable Step

Practice a random act of kindness, either towards yourself or someone else, and observe how it makes you feel.

Take a moment to look at how far you have come and celebrate every aspect of your journey. Your determination, grit, and perseverance are definitely paying off. Keep moving forward!

# 11 | REWRITING YOUR NARRATIVE: BECOMING THE HERO OF YOUR STORY

*"One day, you will tell your story of how you overcame what you went through and it will be someone else's survival guide."*

—Brené Brown

**What if I told you that the story you've been telling yourself is not the end, but just the beginning?** The pain, the trauma, the heartache—they do not define you. For so long, you may have seen yourself as the victim of circumstances beyond your control, stuck in a narrative that keeps you feeling small, powerless, and unworthy.

But what if, instead of being the victim, you became the hero of your story?

Rewriting your narrative is one of the most powerful steps you can take on your healing journey. It's the moment you decide that your past will no longer dictate your future.

Seeing yourself as a survivor, not a victim, brings empowerment, strength, and clarity. It shifts your mindset from being someone that life happens to, to someone who shapes their own destiny.

When you step into the role of the hero, you reclaim your power, discover your inner strength, and realize that no obstacle or trauma is too great to overcome. You are the author of your own story, and it's time to write a new chapter.

There will be parts of your healing journey when you encounter roadblocks that cause you to come to a complete stop. You will not be able to force these roadblocks out of your mind, or push them out of the road with a bulldozer. They stand with concrete strength, waiting for you to notice them, discover what is beyond them, and clear them out.

This may not be the first time that you have come into contact with this roadblock—you might have dealt with it many times before. However, in order to completely heal the wound, each roadblock requires multiple versions of you to face it as you mature.

These roadblocks have been massive obstacles on your journey. Not knowing that each time you chose to say, "I'll deal with this later" and take a detour, the obstacle would grow bigger and stronger, you have pushed it off until what was once the size of a pea has now become the size of a 10-ton elephant that can't be ignored.

In the past, you always tried to shrug it off and distract yourself so you wouldn't think about it—by bingeing a new show that you don't even care about, scrolling aimlessly on your phone to pass the time, or listening to music so you wouldn't have to sit uncomfortably in silence. Suddenly, nothing you have tried is working, and you are being forced to stop and deal with the issue that you have repeatedly ignored.

The story that you have told yourself for years has weighed you down. It has made that backpack even harder to carry, and at times made you feel like you had shackles around your feet that prevented you from moving anywhere.

For years, you have repeatedly told yourself negative things because of what others led you to believe, until it became a habit you can't seem to break. You have told yourself things such as ….

> *"I'm such a failure. I will never get it right."*
>
> *"I'm so unloveable. No one will ever care about me."*
>
> *"I will never be good enough. I have tried so hard and nothing works for me."*

The list goes on and on. Now, the elephant that you have neglected for so long is sitting on your chest, forcing you to deal with it before you can move. At this point, you do the only thing that you can do—stop everything and deal with it.

Once again, you are being forced to sit in your pain and look at things differently. Little do you know, you are about to massively shift your perspective due to this one action. You are able to rewrite the narrative of your life—the story that was once about a person who always struggled and never thrived, becomes a story about a hero who can take on elephants and live to tell the tale.

At this moment, you start to replay the worst moments of your life. The time when you were left by the person you thought loved you the most, the seconds that felt like a lifetime when someone laid their hands on you to harm you, the moments when you laid in the hospital room alone, waiting to deliver, or those hours you spent pouring yourself into someone else until you had nothing left to give anyone—including yourself.

Maybe it was the moment you had to do the bravest thing and let go of a beloved pet and allow them to cross the Rainbow Bridge so they would no longer suffer, the days when you missed out on time with your kids because you were working hard to provide for them after a divorce, or the moment after the doctor told you your beloved parent had just passed away, when you kissed them on the forehead and rested your head on their chest—where their heart no longer beats.

In all of these moments, time stood still while you clung to it white-knuckled, not even sure how you would maneuver through each experience. You have changed so much from each one of these experiences.

Even though you did not always know what to do or how you were going to do it, you made it through anyway. No, it did not always look like the most beautiful present under the tree wrapped in the comic section from the *Courier-Journal* with a handmade bow, but it did not look like the ugliest one either.

At this point, you have transitioned through so many versions of yourself that the you that steps forward sees things differently than ever before, thinks more positively, and has the ability to flip the script on anything negative because you choose to find the silver lining.

By finding the silver linings, you are able to survive traumatic life experiences, provide love and empathy for people who may never have had it otherwise, and show the true nature of your heart of gold through compassion and kindness.

When you chase away the darkness that once filled your soul, you realize that your determination to live your life on your own terms has improved everything about you.

Where you once trapped in negativity, you are now filled with unconditional love, peace, and patience. These days, you are telling yourself things that sound like:

> *"I may have felt like a failure at times, but I never gave up and consistently showed up for those that matter to me the most. I have learned so much from the times I felt like I failed."*
>
> *"I'm loved beyond measure. The right people will show up and stay, not because of what I do, but because of who I am as a person. I'm surrounded by love everyday."*
>
> *"I am good enough for the people who are meant for me. I know that I will show up and give my best everyday."*
>
> *"I am no longer a victim, but a survivor. Whatever life has thrown at me, I have chosen to navigate the path to the best of my abilities, even if that meant changing into a healthier and happier version of myself."*

When you take the time to flip the script on every negative thing that you have been told or that you have told yourself, you delete the negativity in your own life and replace it with positivity.

In this way, you are no longer the villain in your story, but the hero. You have met every obstacle head on, found a way to empower yourself, and used your out-of-the-box way of thinking to create the solutions to your problems. On the days you felt like you were not only surviving, you were also thriving.

Each version of yourself will have to step up to the plate differently in life. The ways that you choose to face your problems will reflect your resilience, your strength, and the lessons you've learned from every hardship.

Every step forward, no matter how small, is a testament to your courage in the face of adversity. Each new version of yourself shows the depth of your growth and your unwavering determination to rise, no matter the challenges you've endured.

Let's take a moment to look back on all the challenges that you have faced in your life. You will use this as part of your actionable step for this part of your journey. Get ready to remove the roadblocks on your path.

## Actionable Step

Write a short story where you are the hero overcoming the challenges of your life. Focus on your strengths and victories.

When you take a moment to look back at what you have accomplished in the face of adversity, you empower yourself. Revisiting this activity in the moments when you are struggling may help you to see things in a new way and provide gentle, loving care to yourself.

Be proud of everything that you have accomplished—you are meant for so much more in your life. Do not stop now. Keep going!

# 12 | FINDING YOUR VOICE: SPEAKING YOUR TRUTH WITH CONFIDENCE

*"The message behind the words is the voice of the heart."*

—Rumi

There's a moment, after years of silence, where the words sitting in your throat finally fight their way out. That moment is raw, terrifying, and electrifying all at once. It's the first breath of truth you take after holding it in for so long, and in that moment, you begin to find your voice.

Finding your voice means reclaiming the power that was stripped away, the power that lay dormant beneath the fear and pain. Speaking your truth doesn't just change your life—it opens up new paths you hadn't yet dared to walk. It's in this breaking of silence that you start to rewrite your story.

The courage to share your voice doesn't just set you free; it creates space for others to break their own silence, to step forward and rewrite their own narrative.

Your voice, once silenced, now becomes a beacon of strength, not just for yourself, but for anyone seeking the courage to speak their truth and change their lives in ways they never imagined possible.

It starts off as a whisper. *"I have something to say and I need to say it."*

Before now, you have chosen to ignore this whispered voice, because you know that you are the only one who can hear it—it's your inner voice. However, at this point of your healing journey, your inner voice is getting louder and louder and louder until it becomes an internal roar, like a lion no longer willing to be muzzled.

*"I have something to say and I need to say it."*

You start to listen to and acknowledge your inner voice, and you decide you are ready to break your silence. But how? How, after years of being so silent that even a doormouse could not hear you, do you break free and share your voice with the world? Even though you may not know why, you know you need to speak up and share what is in your heart.

*"I have something to say and I need to say it."*

You think of a few ways that you can break your silence without overwhelming yourself and shutting down afterwards. Journaling, talking to a friend, writing some poetry, and talking to yourself out loud …

Nothing feels right. You keep thinking of ways to share your truth that would feel safe enough, but you keep crossing them off in your mind. *"That's not good enough," "that is way too scary,"* and *"I could never do that,"* replay in the back of your mind.

Suddenly, an idea nothing like anything you'd considered before comes unexpectedly. Somehow it found its way to you, and in that moment, that split second, you engaged and shared your truth.

Finding your voice is one thing, while speaking with confidence is another. When you have been silent for years in an effort to protect yourself from judgment and criticism, finding and sharing your voice can be overwhelming to the point of shutting down.

In order to navigate this part of the healing journey, it takes time, patience, and a deep willingness to accept change. You may feel strong enough one day and think, *"Today is the day."*

Other days, you may just want to lie in bed and hope that tomorrow you will feel better. Your journey to finding your voice may be similar to others' experiences, and it may be completely different.

Remember, this is your healing journey. It is unique to you. How it unfolds is the way that it is meant to unfold—no shaming or blaming is needed. Be patient and trust the timing.

Finding your voice is a process that is different for everyone. It may start off as a whisper that speaks to you all the time. Or it might also only speak to you when your mind is still and your thoughts are quiet.

You may have started to find your voice during a poetry writing session when you began to touch your deep inner wounds, or when you were practicing a speech for an upcoming meeting.

You may have started to find your voice while preparing to give your final speech on a class project, marking another accomplishment complete. You may have realized that it felt odd to speak, that your voice did not sound like your own, or that the internal sensation you felt was anything but comforting.

When you first heard the voice that had been trapped inside its cage for what felt like forever, it may have sounded weak—unlike the scream that you thought it would elicit.

*"It sounded nothing like I thought it would."*

While you would like to go back and put your voice back in its box, you know that isn't a possibility. Something inside you is pushing you forward. Sometimes it even feels more like a forceful shove. So, you continue to push forward even amongst all the strangeness.

After you start to share your voice in other aspects of your life, you realize that more opportunities are showing up for you to break your silence about what has happened to you. Your traumas, the things that you have held so tightly and close to your heart, even when you were experiencing uncontrollable pain. *"I just wish that it would stop."*

After you start to share your voice in other aspects of your life, you realize that more opportunities are showing up for you to break your silence about what has happened to you. You find yourself ready to speak about the traumas you've kept hidden, the experiences you've guarded so closely, and the unbearable amounts of pain and darkness that you have survived.

Previously, you would have turned right back around and put your voice back in its box without question, but this is a new version of you who is facing fears and overcoming obstacles.

Your strong internal drive to move forward is allowing you to cross paths that you would have never dreamed of navigating. In this space, you have gained wisdom, serenity, grace, and the ability to know when it's safe enough to push forward, and when it's time for you to rest to prevent burnout.

Once you find your voice, using it to speak with confidence is not far away—although it may feel like it is. By continuously stepping up to the plate and doing things that you would not normally do, you are showing yourself that you are confident in your abilities—including speaking your truth.

Once you catch a glimmer of the internal confidence that you possess, it will start to show itself outwardly when you speak. Your voice will no longer sound weak or different to you, but like the voice you heard before all of the traumatic experiences that took place in your life.

You will no longer worry about when to speak or what to say when you do, but you will feel comfortable enough to speak at any time that you need to. This will also help when your needs are going unmet.

Finding your voice with confidence also means that you can show up as your own best advocate. No one can speak for you like you do. You have always known yourself the best (even when you decided to believe in the lies that others were telling you).

Whether you are sharing your voice for the first time, or after a long period of silence, you are deciding to change the trajectory of your life. You are stepping up in a way that you have never felt comfortable enough to step up before.

You also know that growth does not happen when you are comfortable. It happens when you are uncomfortable and scared to navigate the change, but you choose to do it anyway.

Be proud of yourself in this moment, no matter how your voice sounds to you. When you have chosen to share, it may also be the day that someone else needs to hear what you have to say in order to get past their own struggles.

Sharing your voice allows you the space to show up authentically. No longer will you feel like you need to say things that will get the approval of the room. You will stand surely and strongly in your truth.

You may still feel strange at times—even when you are confident—but when people acknowledge you and thank you for sharing your truth, you will know that you've started a ripple of change in the world and further inspired others to share their own truth.

Deep and true connections start with vulnerability and by embracing fear. You will continue to overcome years of adversity as you bravely share your voice with confidence.

## Actionable Step

Practice speaking your truth in a safe setting. This could be with a trusted friend, therapist, or even in front of a mirror.

Remember, be patient, kind, and trusting of the process. Your voice may sound unfamiliar to you at first—this is ok. It is, in fact, normal. When I first shared my voice, I felt the same way. It took some time to get used to hearing myself talk to others when I had been so used to talking to myself.

As time moves forward, you will get comfortable with speaking and sharing your voice again, and as you do your confidence will soar. You've got this!

# 13 | THE ART OF LETTING GO: FREEING YOURSELF FROM THE PAST

*"The beautiful journey of today can only begin when we learn to let go of yesterday."*

—Steve Maraboli

Letting go is perhaps one of the most courageous acts of healing—a deliberate choice to release the past that you've clung to so tightly, it's become part of your very identity.

You've held onto memories for years, some that once filled your lungs with the fresh air of joy, and others that seemed to choke the very essence of your being. Carrying this weight is like trudging through the airport with luggage that should have been checked at the ticket counter, each step more exhausting than the last, leaving you breathless and wondering if you'll ever reach your gate.

But imagine just for a moment, setting that luggage down—feeling the immediate relief, the lightness, the surge of energy as you stand taller and breathe easier.

The art of letting go is exactly this: freeing yourself from the burdens that no longer serve you, so you can move forward unencumbered, ready to embrace sights and experiences more beautiful than you ever imagined.

It's about creating a safe space within yourself to breathe with ease, to let happiness seep back in, and to rediscover the person you were always meant to be.

In letting go, you don't lose the positive memories that lifted you; instead, you honor them while bravely discarding the ones that have held you back, stepping into a future defined not by your past, but by the limitless possibilities ahead.

For a very long time, you have felt as though your past has defined you, especially as you have stumbled and fallen in an effort to survive. Everything that you do at this moment reminds you of your past—the way that you speak, how you carry yourself, the things that you wear, and the way you wait to speak until you are spoken to.

You have never really known yourself without these memories, and the truest version of you has been smothered by the safety blankets that used to protect you. You start to wonder what life would look like on the other side—a place where your past memories no longer hold you hostage and you feel free.

Life has always felt like it just happened to you, with no control on your part. At times, you even asked yourself, *"Why do I even exist, anyway?"* You did your best to navigate every storm, even when you were too cold and soaking wet to care anymore.

Everything you tried felt like it failed. Every fear you had seemed to come true. You always did your best to think positively, hoping that the bad thoughts would take a detour on the next exit, but it never seemed to happen for you.

Despite all the positivity, love, and care that you infused into others, life responded in the most negative and cold ways. At times, it felt like you were knocking on doors in a blizzard, hoping that someone would come and rescue you. That never happened.

In between each disaster, you stepped up to the plate and saved yourself. You became your own hero and rewrote the script that you were given: one about a girl who would never amount to anything, and would always remain weak in the eye of adversity. Deep down, you knew this script was not about you, so you did your best to overcome every obstacle on your path. Somehow, you always made it work for you.

Now, you are considering your life without the debilitating coldness of negative memories. This is a process that you haven't thought of before, because you thought that you would carry those memories around forever.

You choose to replay memories that feel warm and wrap you in unconditional love, and compare them to the negative memories that were bleak and cold. You take time between each memory to notice how you are feeling.

In an effort to connect with yourself on a deeper level, you start to brainstorm on two different pieces of paper, one page titled "positivity" and the other titled "negativity." Within minutes, you've filled both pages. Your heart begins to open up to the possibility of living life with positivity. You have made your choice.

Taking the time to reconnect with your memories, both positive and negative, can be an overwhelming experience. In fact, it may even require you to take extra time to process memories that you may have forgotten or have chosen to ignore. This is ok. Take all the time you need, and allow yourself to feel the emotions that you have repressed.

When you are able to notice how you are feeling, name the emotion that is occurring, and feel safe enough to press forward, it means that you are ready for the next step on your healing journey: letting go and freeing yourself from the past.

You have carried these heavy burdens for so long, and now you are ready to put them down and free yourself of their weight. You want to make life easier, navigate a new path, and breathe fresh and clean air.

You want to live life freely, with emotional stability. Now that you see another option, you are no longer willing to struggle. You are now ready to embark on a new path that is opening up in front of your very eyes.

Once you get started on this path, it's like you have your foot on the accelerator ready to get to your next destination. At the beginning, things are slow, dark, and miserable as you process your negative memories and let them go.

You have taken the time to look at each painful memory and learn from it, so you know what to do should the same situation replay itself. You have cried your eyes out to the point of them being red, glassy, and swollen, and you've gone through so many boxes of tissues that you have lost count.

When you are home, you feel safe and protected, but you feel naked in society, even though you are completely clothed. Instead of hiding inside, you continue to go outside in an effort to embrace the world around you, hoping that it will embrace you back.

This part of the path is hard, and forces you to dig deeper and believe in your abilities to get through it. In time, things will get easier, and everything that you are going through now will start to make sense.

You'll start to hear songs on the radio that you have heard before, only certain lyrics will stand out in your mind. You'll notice that something that you had just thought of that was positive, you'll start to read about it in the days to come. Somehow, in this moment, everything feels like it is starting to align for you.

Songs you've heard countless times suddenly reveal lyrics that speak directly to your journey. Positive thoughts you hold begin appearing in unexpected places—in books you randomly open, conversations you overhear, or articles that cross your path. These synchronicities multiply when you stop living by others' expectations and start flowing with your own truth. In these moments, you feel the pieces of your life clicking into place, each small coincidence confirming that you're exactly where you need to be.

Even though you might once have considered them nightmares, the dreams that you are having now will show you how to navigate this new path. Starting on any new path feels like you are waiting for the ground to fall away from your feet, but you continue to walk down the path anyway. Each time you take a step, you feel more surefooted, and what once looked blurry is now clear as a sunny spring morning.

When you re-examine your memories, you can reconnect with, but also fall in love with yourself completely—maybe for the first time in your life. The person in the mirror smiles back when you smile at her.

Now that you are being completely honest with yourself about how you are feeling at any given moment, your mind is opening to change—and this part of the healing journey has certainly changed you for the better. Though it was difficult in the beginning, you have finally learned to embrace yourself and all that life has to offer you.

Continue to show up for yourself in ways that you never imagined, and watch all the opportunities that flow your way—this is you living your life in alignment.

## Actionable Step

Create a "letting go" list, detailing the emotions, memories, or situations you are ready to release. Reflect on how this will lighten your journey forward.

What you wish to do with your list after you create it is up to you. Be completely honest here and hide nothing from yourself. This is where you learn to dig deeper and trust the ever-evolving process.

## 14 | RISING FROM THE ASHES: THE PHOENIX WITHIN

> *"Self-transformation is not just about changing yourself.*
> *It means shifting yourself to a completely new dimension*
> *of experience and perception."*
>
> —Jaggi Vasudev

The journey of healing from trauma can feel like you're walking through fire, wondering how much more you must endure before you finally feel safe. At times, it seems to burn through the deepest corners of your mind—places you've tried so hard to lock away in order to survive. It's treacherous, pulling at memories you thought you'd forgotten, forcing you to confront the pain you spent years burying.

In those moments, when the weight of it all makes you feel stuck, like there's no clear path forward, you may question whether you can keep going. You're constantly putting out fires that others started, while desperately trying to hold onto whatever remains of your peace and sanity.

This journey feels like living multiple lives within one—a cycle of shedding who you were in order to embrace who you are becoming. Each time you rise again, you do so with a little more wisdom, leaving behind the broken pieces of your old self like ashes from a fire.

Just like the Phoenix, you rise stronger, bolder, and living on your own terms. This time, everything has changed, and this new life is yours to define.

You have suffered through pain so deep and overwhelming that you have questioned how you are still here. You have fought your internal demons that terrorize you relentlessly and repeat thoughts that would make many people run and hide.

Your intrusive thoughts have been dark and scary, and at times you are afraid of what you will do if someone attempts to harm you in the ways you have been harmed before.

Even the thought of certain triggers occurring causes you to go into a rage where your senses feel so heightened and hyper-aware that the slightest movement makes your head spin. These days your head is on a swivel—constantly searching for the next fire to put out.

Recently, the fires you have been putting out have been starting rapidly and with fury. You thought you had everything figured out and could finally rest for a bit, but suddenly, you felt like you were back in that relationship where everything was your responsibility, even though there were two people that could handle it.

You fought so hard to free yourself from this relationship so you could be happy and find who you truly are again. You lost yourself several times in that space, and even though your surroundings have changed and you have not been in contact with that person in years, at this moment, you feel like you are back there.

Leaving that situation helped you to gain the space that you needed in order to free your mind and heal your deepest wounds. But lately, those wounds have opened back up.

You recently saw your bank account in the red, which was a constant in your joint account during that relationship. You wonder if you will be able to continue to provide for your family, including those fuzzy four-legged individuals who have provided you with all the support you could ever need.

You question your current reality, wondering what it is trying to teach you this time—you thought that you had already learned these lessons. You are hitting your breaking point, and you're not sure how much more you can handle. Lately, you have been short-fused, and when you speak you are stating exactly how you feel.

Life has certainly been breathtakingly interesting! You had no idea what you were in for when you finally decided to make yourself a priority and deep dive into your healing journey.

You knew that it would not be easy, but you had dealt with enough brokenness and heartache that you were ready to forge onward to a new journey that would take you to places you had never seen.

You used to cling to anyone who paid attention to you even when they treated you poorly, but on this journey, you learned that some people were meant to stay and others had to go.

You thought love meant doing things to be appreciated, instead of being valued for who you are. You thought you understood finances well enough, until your significant other who spent uncontrollably took you for a ride with your joint account.

You were expected from a young age to be the nice woman who always said "yes," but sometimes being the nice one was so tiring and fake.

*"I just want to be who I was always meant to be."*

The woman you are now is not the woman you were when you embarked on this healing journey. True, you have had overwhelming losses and have fought to the very depths to hold onto what is most dear to you, but you have also enriched your knowledge and wisdom along the way.

You have been able to embrace life on different terms even when you were still trying to figure it out for yourself. Previously, the thought of being alone terrified you, but now it's something you look forward to. Being alone with your thoughts and feelings allows you to connect with yourself on a deeper level and find the necessary steps to move forward.

Even though it feels like everything is falling apart and you are ready to scream, you know that you have the tools to put things back into place. During this healing journey, you have been courageous, steadfast, and tackled things that you would have never handled before.

You have also learned to be kind, patient, and gentle with yourself, especially when you are struggling the most. No longer do you continue to push yourself to the point of exhaustion and burnout, but instead you take the time you need to rest and replenish. You have learned so much about caring for yourself along this healing journey.

At one point, you would have accepted whatever was thrown your way, including the person who you knew deep down was not right for you. You settled for jobs that you were not happy with and allowed dead end positions to stagnate your internal growth. You would work overtime when asked, because you felt like you couldn't say "no" to anything.

Now things have changed dramatically. You are no longer willing to accept someone who is not right for you, a dead-end job where you aren't appreciated or respected, or anything else that causes your growth to halt and depreciates your self-care.

When the fires are rising around you again, you are quick to put them out. Your traumatic experiences have given you the ability to think on your feet, coming up with out-of-the-box solutions to overcome adversity.

Things may feel the same, but the way that you react and respond has greatly changed. You start to realize just how much knowledge you have gained on your healing journey. You can smile and breathe with ease as you hear yourself say, *"I can do this."*

For years, you remained silent, trying to protect the things that made you feel the most vulnerable because you were afraid of what people would think of you.

Now, you openly state how you feel, ask for what you need, and stand up for what you truly believe in. Speaking your truth has certainly been stressful at times, but finally, you are starting to feel comfortable with being who you were always meant to be. Settling for anything less than you deserve is a thing of the past!

During your healing journey, you repeatedly experienced death to the parts of you that you held so tightly, afraid that if you let them go you would lose yourself.

You have learned that it was necessary to let go of these parts of you, because they had fulfilled their role and you no longer needed them. The "yes" girl, the silent one, the one who only speaks when spoken to, the one who showed no emotion other than happiness, the therapist friend, the one who has it all together, and all the other versions of you that helped you arrive at this point in your life.

While those parts are no longer needed today, they helped you to survive all the storms of your life. Be grateful for these parts of you that once existed, as they have helped to set you free.

Fires may come and go, and you have learned how to put them out quickly. The woman who has seen so much now stands unshaken, equipped with strength forged in the heat of those flames.

You no longer fear the blaze because you know that with each fire, you will rise stronger, more resilient, and more empowered than before. You are not defined by the fires that burn around you, but by the unbreakable spirit that continues to rise from the ashes.

Life has tested you and your ability to resolve great conflicts, but due to your determination, willpower, strength, and drive to move forward, you have arrived at this very moment a whole new you.

## Actionable Step

You will use a different tool from your backpack for this actionable step—visualization.

Visualize your transformation and draw or write about what your "Phoenix" self looks like. What qualities have emerged from your journey?

This is a great actionable step to use during the times when you feel stuck and think that nothing has changed. Comparing where you were to where you are now will help you dial into yourself and see how much things have really changed for the better.

Be proud of how far you have come on your healing journey and celebrate yourself!

# 15 | TURNING SCARS INTO STARS: THE ART OF TRANSFORMATION

*"Growth and self-transformation cannot be delegated."*

—Lewis Mumford

There were days when the scars from your past felt too deep to ever heal. The hurtful words from those you thought loved you, the family members who let you down when you needed them the most, and all the painful moments in between, seemed to etch themselves into your soul. The scars were so tightly woven into your heart that they drained the very life out of you, constant reminders of your pain even when you thought you'd finally moved on. But scars tell a story.

They aren't just remnants of your suffering—they are proof that you survived. What once oozed with anger and pain has slowly transformed into something powerful, a symbol of resilience and strength. These scars are no longer wounds; they are stars—guiding you forward, lighting the way, and reminding you of how far you've come.

There is no doubt that you have struggled and clawed your way to get where you are today. The journey from then until now isn't something that you ever thought you would have experienced, but here you stand today, changed by the very essence of it.

When you started on this path, you had no idea what was in store for you, but you knew something had to change and you were the only one who could do it. Life has been an emotional rollercoaster—at times, you showed up feeling like you had it all together, but other times, you felt messy and despondent. Despite life's ups and downs, you made sure you consistently showed up ready to embrace the experience.

Along the way, you have had to heal many wounds. Some wounds were small, with hardly any healing time at all. Then there were the wounds that were large, wide open, and seeping fluid, so that as hard as you tried, there was just no way to heal them without an infection or two first.

Your wounds became infected when you continued to repeat patterns that you told yourself you would break. You vowed, *"Just one more time. This time will be different than the last."*

But it was always the same as before—the only exception was that you knew the red flags to look out for, but you chose to ignore them, thinking if you just added some extra love and gave a little more, everything would be ok. Man, were you wrong about that.

You decided to try anyway, in an effort to prove to yourself that at some point, the infections from your past wounds would stop. Instead, the wounds grew larger, into gaping holes that no amount of stitching would fix. You would have to let the wound heal from the inside out. This required you to do something that you had never done before: take time to yourself, process what had happened, feel your emotions, and set yourself free.

You took it a few steps farther, making yourself a priority and learning how to provide for your unmet needs that you had always neglected to care for others.

Once you started being completely honest with yourself and stopped the shame and blame routine, your needs made themselves known. When you prioritized yourself and began to meet your needs, the gaping wounds started to heal.

As your wounds healed, you gained wisdom that you would not have learned had you not taken the time to care for yourself. You learned to actively listen to your needs and figured out ways to meet them, even when the rest of your life is busy and stressful.

You found that having quiet time to yourself was nourishing and refreshing to your heart. You learned how to state how you truly felt and to match your words to your emotions, and to speak freely and truthfully at any given moment. Living authentically helped your wounds heal faster than you ever thought possible.

Turns out, in order to heal your wounds from their infections, your heart and soul needed the same amount of love, attention, appreciation, patience, and kindness that you had so easily given to others. You have had these abilities all along, but you believed you had to meet the needs of others before you could meet your own.

In the time that you spent alone, you realized that the exact opposite is true—you have to provide for yourself first before you can provide for others. This thought was very foreign to you at first—you felt that if you put yourself first, it would mean you were selfish. Now, you know that this is far from the truth.

Providing yourself with the care you need so badly on a daily basis has closed the infected wounds into healed scars that adorn your heart and soul. No longer weighing you down with the darkness of the past, they have become stars that shine brightly while you are out in the world.

These stars, born from pain, now illuminate your path forward, guiding you toward a life filled with purpose, love, and resilience. Each star tells the story of your transformation, a testament to your strength, and a reminder that you are capable of turning even the deepest wounds into sources of light and beauty.

As you continue to care for yourself, these stars grow brighter, empowering you to step into the world with confidence, knowing that you are whole, worthy, and unbreakable.

## Actionable Step

Let's take a moment to reflect on a past wound that has become a source of strength. Write down how it has shaped who you are today and how it can guide your future.

# 16 | REDEFINING YOURSELF: BEYOND THE PAIN

*"It's never too late to become who you want to be. You have the power within to start over."*

—F. Scott Fitzgerald

It's so easy to get stuck in your pain, to allow your trauma to define who you are and what your life will be. The world feels cruel, the weight unbearable, and the label of "victim" clings to you like a second skin.

It can seem like life's against you, leaving you powerless and disconnected from joy, love, and trust. But what if, in the midst of this darkness, you made the brave choice to see yourself differently? To decide, right now, that your pain will no longer be the lens through which you view your life?

You have the power to rewrite your story, to rise beyond the limitations placed on you, and to reclaim the identity that's been waiting for you all along. Trauma does not define you unless you allow it.

By sitting with your pain, processing your emotions, and choosing to learn from the past, you open the door to a life that is yours to shape—a life beyond the pain, where you are not just a survivor, but an unbreakable warrior.

Having a victim's mindset reminds you to stay small, not to speak at all, and to stay in your protective bubble without allowing it to pop. Your rose colored glasses have disintegrated, and you now see the world through a very bleak lens of brown murky overtones.

Living life through this lens encourages self-deprecation, as you doubt your value, and believe that there is nothing good left for you. Your intrusive thoughts make you continuously question, *"Why am I even here, anyway?"*

Despite the overwhelming pain that you feel on a daily basis, you continue to show up—even when you feel messy. Your internal world is pitch black, and you can barely see the flickering light that still shines within you. The external world has no color, with no joy to be felt or love to be seen.

You're trying your best to balance your internal and external worlds, but nothing seems to be able to motivate you to move forward. You feel trapped and stagnant in this moment, not sure if you have any good days left to show up for. You know that you have done the work to overcome so much, yet everything still seems the same. *"There has to be something else that I am missing ... "*

Your pain has followed you for years and has become a deeply enmeshed part of your soul. You thought that taking the time to sit in your pain, feel your emotions, and be honest with yourself would be the ticket to change.

Turns out, that is only part of it. The other part is letting go of what no longer serves you—the victim mindset. While this mindset has helped protect you, it has also alienated you from the things that you want the most. Deep and meaningful connections, trusted relationships, and a love so pure and honest that it would make your soul blush.

You hide behind the victim mindset because you thought it was serving you, but as you move forward in an effort to rid yourself of your pain, what once acted as a safety blanket is now shielding you from the things you desire.

*"I am no longer a victim. I am a survivor."*

You have made extraordinary efforts to process and heal your pain, closing wounds that you thought would remain open and oozing forever. Through your willpower, you have overcome the things you used to think you could not do.

You start to see how much things have really changed for the better, and you are able to flip the script on your painful past by telling yourself, *"I have been able to accomplish so much. I can do more to feel better and be better."*

You start to look past your pain and begin to see that love is present. Instead of continuing to carry the resentment, hate, and rage, you choose to set that heavy baggage down. You start to feel a little better and take your next steps forward. Part of letting go of the victim mindset is the willingness to embrace the mindset of a survivor, which can free you further from your pain.

The survivor mindset empowers you to choose to live life on your own terms and fully experience freedom. It gives you the peace of mind to discard the murky, brown-colored glasses and see your pain and traumas as stepping stones to a brighter, more colorful future full of love, joy, and trust.

When you first shed the victim mindset and see the world in beautiful, full-spectrum color, you'll breathe a sigh of relief. In this space, you'll feel fearless and free.

During times of self-doubt and low self-worth, you may notice that the murky brown world starts to return. When this happens, take some time to restructure your thoughts in a positive manner, and remind yourself of a few of the things that you have accomplished.

As you begin this change, your mind may still try to play tricks on you. Training it to become your ally will help you overcome this setback and turn it into a comeback.

Becoming the author of your story breathes new life into your lungs, love into your heart, and frees your soul. You are allowed to see past your pain instead of continuously living it.

Although you were previously a slave to your mind, you have finally set yourself free. You have also gained more tools to add to your backpack—empowerment, strength, and resilience. These tools have been with you all along.

On your worst days, they have allowed you to dig a little deeper to find the next stepping stones on your healing journey. Bolstering your internal resolve and reminding you that you can do anything you put your mind to, these tools have shown you the path to overcoming blocks in the road. The great thing is these problem-solving tools are with you to stay and will help you to live beyond your pain.

The light that was once a small flicker is now a brilliant flame shining bright inside you, ready to light the way through your pain. It has always been there with you, even when you struggled the most. The depths of your pain and suffering were no match for this light as it helped to guide you over all the stumbling blocks.

Each time you overcame an obstacle, the light inside you flickered and danced and guided you further along the path home. Being able to live beyond your pain is a true testament to the woman that you are—strong, resilient, and vibrant, with the ability to turn pain into power!

## Actionable Step

Write a personal mission statement that reflects your new, empowered identity. What values, goals, and principles will guide your life moving forward?

Your personal mission statement can be anything that you want it to be. It is meant to help you create an internal alignment to the things that matter to you the most—your values, goals, and principles. These are just a few of the things that we work on in my course *Finding Direction from Within.*

This course was created to help women with a history of trauma to develop self-confidence, self-love, and peace of mind, so if you're interested in learning more about it, please reach out to me at gina@ginahamiltoncoaching.com so that we can connect. I look forward to hearing from you soon!

## 17 | FROM SURVIVING TO THRIVING: CREATING YOUR NEW NORMAL

*"As you move outside of your comfort zone, what was once the unknown and frightening becomes your new normal."*

—Robin S. Sharma

For so long, survival has been your primary instinct. You were barely treading water, doing whatever was necessary to get through each day. You hid your voice, blended in with your surroundings like a chameleon, and even gaslit yourself to numb the pain. These survival tactics kept you alive, but they were never the true essence of who you are.

The person you became in the midst of trauma was forged in the fires of necessity, a version of yourself built to adapt to a hostile world. Now, as you step out of the storm, you are faced with a new challenge: not just surviving, but thriving.

It's time to shed your armor, to dismantle the false personas you created out of fear and self-preservation, and to build a new normal where you can fully live, love, and flourish.

The journey ahead is about discovering who you are and creating a life that feels truly, authentically yours. The parts of you that you created to survive your traumatic experiences were never who you truly were. You created them in a hostile environment, in order to feel a little safer, more known, and somewhat comfortable, so you could continue to exist instead of surrendering at the feet of your mortal enemy.

You tried to pave the way to freedom and true authentic self-expression, even while continuing to hide who you really were. You did your best to find situations that would be better than the last, only to end up in the same situation with a new person and surroundings. Life felt like a repetitive cycle, and your head felt like it was just taken out of a washer stuck on the spin cycle.

At one point, you finally got tired of repeating unhealthy patterns. You started to pay more attention to them and vowed to make changes that would stick.

It wasn't until you started to do this on a regular basis that things began to change. When you made the intentional decision to make yourself a priority and to enrich your life in the same ways that you had done for others, everything shifted.

You finally started to feel sturdy and balanced on your feet, and you felt a sense of peace that you had never felt before. You realized you were moving beyond just surviving, and finally learning to thrive.

Thriving feels safe, like a hoodie on a crisp fall evening. Your thoughts are positive and creative like your favorite cartoon, and your outlook on life is full of unconditional love and acceptance.

You have finally started to find the aspects of life that you always craved. When something disrupts your peace, you are able to quickly change the narrative and your surroundings and return to your peaceful existence. When you think back on what your life was, you realize that so much has changed, and the storms you once faced are over.

You used to dream about what your life would look like in a safe and free space, where you could be your own person and you would no longer be shackled by toxic people.

You have fought long and hard to get where you are today, and have broken through every obstacle set to throw you off course. You have finally created the life of your dreams, knowing that no one can take it away from you unless you let them.

You feel more secure in your relationships, allowing people in your life to come and go instead of struggling to hold on tight to keep them. This has given you a new sense of freedom where people stay because they truly want to, and not because they are forced to—due to your actions or theirs.

Life seems to be flowing towards you, and navigating it feels effortless and free. You finally feel able to breathe with ease, and you can move in a way that feels right to you. Because your path has been different and unique, you have been able to create a meaningful and connected life on your own terms.

Along the path, you have learned about yourself on a deeper level. Before, you didn't pay attention to what you value, the things that you are passionate about, and your deep inner drive to keep pushing toward your goals. At times, they were lost among your surroundings and the people who were most toxic to you.

When you took time away to heal, you were able to find them again. You realized that by connecting with your values, passions, and goals, you could live in alignment with who you truly are.

Shedding the skin from your traumas, breaking repetitive patterns, and letting go of the things that no longer serve you has greatly freed you from your previous life of pain.

Even the way you move around the world has changed. You used to hang your head as you walked around, staring at the ground. Now you walk with your head held high, showing your deep inner confidence.

Life has not always been easy, but you have done your best to make the necessary changes to not only survive, but to thrive.

While on this path, the things that are important to you have also begun to change. You know that this is because you are leaving your comfort zone more often, in order to embrace growth and self-improvement.

Because of your perseverance, hard work, and dedication, abundance has arrived in your life in a way that you have never imagined possible.

Let's look at your path and determine some simple and manageable steps that you can take to ensure that you continue to survive and thrive.

## Actionable Step

Identify three changes you can make to your daily routine that will help you move from surviving to thriving. Commit to implementing these changes.

Remember to be patient, loving, and kind to yourself with any type of change. Change takes time and does not normally occur overnight. If you try something and realize that it is not working, give yourself permission to make adaptations to the new change or let that one go and try something new.

There is no right or wrong here. Do what is best for you and what feels right in your heart.

# 18 | THE POWER OF CHOICE: CREATING THE LIFE YOU DESERVE

*"The more decisions that you are forced to make alone, the more you are aware of your freedom to choose."*

—Thornton Wilder

For too long, the power to make your own choices seemed foreign, like a distant luxury you were never afforded. Instead, you've lived under the weight of others' decisions, feeling trapped in a life shaped by someone else's beliefs, desires, and demands. The illusion of autonomy was often dangled before you, only for you to realize that none of the choices truly belonged to you.

Now, as you step out of the shadows of control and into your own light, the realization hits: you have the power to choose your own path. With that power, endless possibilities unfurl before you. No longer confined to a life dictated by others, you can see that each decision you make has the potential to shape the life you've always deserved—one filled with freedom, joy, and peace.

This is your moment to pause, breathe, and take back the reins of your destiny. You no longer need to rush your decisions or make them out of fear. They are yours, waiting to be crafted by your mind and guided by your heart.

Before now, you lived your life based on what everyone else expected of you and not the dreams that you had for yourself. Often, you were given an "opportunity" to make a decision only to be told that it did not sound at all like a choice.

Hearing this every time you made a decision made you question yourself, and you wondered if you could ever make the right choice. The thing is this: you were making the right decisions for yourself, but they were not the decisions the other person wanted you to make.

Instead, this "opportunity" was given to you in order to control you. The choices you made would later be used to manipulate you into doing only what would benefit the other individual, creating an internal disconnect and causing you to abandon yourself.

After not having this luxury in your life, it can be difficult to navigate making decisions and having the ability to choose. It's overwhelmingly scary because you continue to question if what you are doing is right and if it will work out the way that you hoped.

Before, you were never allowed to follow through on your decisions, so you did not get to see the outcome and determine if it was the right one for you. This adds to your fear of making the right decisions.

Making decisions in a slow and steady fashion is the best way to go. Rushed decisions often lead to mistakes and require additional work to return back to stability. Be patient with yourself. Learning to make your own decisions takes patience and practice.

The thing about decisions is that you can make a choice, then take some time to make sure it is the right one for you. If you aren't sure where to go, brainstorming can be a helpful addition to any decision-making process.

Start by using the notes app in your phone or using a pen and piece of paper. At the top, write down what you are trying to make a decision about. You can also write down what you hope to accomplish by making this decision. This will help you maintain focus on what really matters to you as the decision-making process unfolds.

After you have completed those steps, you can start to create a list of the positives and negatives (also called a pros and cons list) to help you figure out what options are available to you as you are making your decision.

Your pros and cons list will help you to figure out two main things: 1) Whether you are interested in the opportunity or not, and 2) What is the best option for this opportunity?

Take, for example, a decision about going out to eat with a friend.

> **Decision**: Should I go out to eat with a friend?
>
> **What I hope to accomplish**: Being ok enough to go out on my own, starting to gain trust and comfort in public, making my own decisions, creating and maintaining a deeper connection.

> **Pros**: Time out with someone I trust and care about, getting out of my routine, connecting with someone and hearing about what they have going on, I normally have an enjoyable time with them, I'm hungry and interested in eating something different than I normally eat.
>
> **Cons**: I'm worried I don't have enough time, I have been having issues with anxiety when I leave the house and I don't know if it will affect me today. My mood is not the greatest as I have been in my head a lot, and I don't know what to wear.
>
> **Based on the above**—Am I interested in going or not?
>
> **Choices**: If I am interested, what time are we going? Where are we eating? If I'm not interested, I need to let them know. Is another day an option?
>
> **Best option**: I'm interested. I need to contact them and let them know so we can schedule when and where to meet.

While this seems like a very simple decision to make, when you have not been able to make your own decisions at all, it can seem rather daunting. The process appears to take an overwhelming amount of time as you work towards connecting with yourself to figure out what is right for you.

When you are able to look at decisions as opportunities to enrich your life, this process also becomes easier. You may even notice that you do not have to use this process anymore because some choices are an automatic yes or no.

If you start to feel stressed about having to tell someone your decision, reach out to them and let them know that you are thinking about it and state when you will contact them. This will help to decrease stress and pressure while also openly communicating with others who are a part of the plan.

Learning to make your own decisions can seem treacherous at first, since you can't follow your choices all the way through and see what the outcome is. You can always make the best decision from your heart and let it guide you through the process.

There are going to be some decisions that you may make that end up worse than you thought. This is certainly ok. The important thing is that you are not beating and shaming yourself about the decision that you made, but instead, you are willing to learn something new about the opportunity and yourself during the process. Most likely, the same situation will occur again, and next time, you will instinctively know what decision is the right one for you.

Developing a response to an opportunity is not a waste of time, as it allows you space to think and come to the decision that is right for you. There are some decisions that you will make that will be automatic, and you will not have to think about them at all.

Then, there will be other decisions that take more time than you had originally thought, and you might question if you are doing the right thing. Fear may strike at this time. Acknowledge the fear for what it is and step forward knowing that you are making the right decision for your heart.

This often occurs when you are trying to take a step in a whole new direction: leaving an abusive relationship, creating and putting into place healthy boundaries, accepting a new job opportunity, making changes to your normal routine.

When you have the ability to make decisions led by your heart, you also have the opportunity to build the life you have always dreamt of.

There are no more rushed decisions unless you put pressure on yourself to do so. There is no one else telling you that what you have chosen to do is not the right thing—it is the right thing by you.

Not everyone will make the same decisions as you—this is ok. Your life is based on how you choose to live it, especially during and after the healing journey.

The luxury of choices and decision making has now become a part of your life and is here to stay. The question is …

What choices are you willing to make so that you can live the life that you have always dreamt of?

Your life has been waiting for you to step up to the plate and design it in the ways that you see fit so that you can live confidently, with self-love and peace of mind. Make the decisions that are best for you that are crafted by your mind and led by your heart.

## Actionable Step

Make a list of areas in your life where you want to make different choices. Outline the first steps you can take toward making those changes.

Remember, there are no right or wrong decisions here. Please be patient, loving, and kind with yourself during this process. Give yourself time to step away from the process when you start to feel overwhelmed so that peace can return to you.

# 19 | UNBROKEN: THE JOURNEY TO SELF-LOVE

*"You yourself, as much as anybody in the entire universe, deserve your love and affection."*

—Buddha

For the majority of your life, you believed that love was something earned by giving it away, endlessly pouring from your heart into others. You became a wellspring of affection for everyone around you, never stopping to ask if you, too, were deserving of that same love. Somewhere along the way, you mistook love for something you had to seek from others—a gift that those you held closest had to grant.

Those you cherished left you feeling hollow, unwanted, or even told you, "You're too much," or "No one will ever love you like I do?" These words were daggers, cutting into your very soul and leaving you questioning if you would ever be loved the way you so deeply desired.

Until one day, the truth quietly found you: love wasn't something you had to chase or beg for. It was already inside you. When you started to love yourself as fiercely as you loved others, you began the journey toward reclaiming your heart. The path to self-love had finally begun.

The types of love that you have experienced before made your once warm and loving heart turn cold and freeze over and made you question everything there was to question about love.

When you gave freely, you were expected to give everything of yourself to the point of exhaustion and deprivation. Instead of respect or appreciation, everything that you did was scrutinized.

When you took time to buy a heart-warming gift, it wasn't enough and it was turned away. When you were interested in intimacy with your special someone, they left you feeling cold, isolated, and with unmet needs.

You always gave your love, but it never seemed to be reciprocated in ways that touched your heart. Something always felt off, and when you tried to close the deficit, it instead grew larger.

Everything that you tried to patch up the problems never seemed to work, and if it did, it wasn't for very long. You would scratch your head, come up with a different solution, and apply those answers to the problem, but it continued to repeat itself. No matter what you tried, nothing worked, and the more that you gave of yourself, the less you received.

You were always available for them. While you had hoped they would provide the same availability to you—they did not. The effort that you put into any relationship that you entered into—friendship or romance—was undeniable, but no matter how much loyalty, support, and care you gave, it was always in question.

In the beginning, these relationships were beautiful to you, and what you thought you always wanted—hope, love, support, and stability, with some added comfort. Until you realized that your emotions, like riding a roller coaster for the first time, were full of extreme highs and lows. But while a roller coaster is thrilling and quickly over, these emotional extremes never seem to end.

*"Someone get me off this ride!"*

As familiar patterns resurfaced in your relationships, you began to see things differently. You realized that maybe you were not the problem all along. Instead, you were ignoring the red flags that indicated that this relationship may not have been meant for you in the first place. No matter what you did or gave up for them, you would never be enough for this person who was also not enough for you.

Then, one day, in the blink of an eye, everything changed. This person, who you had been there for consistently, stopped responding to you and disappeared from your life. Afraid, you wondered what you needed to do to get them back. You thought of new solutions that you had not tried before, hoping that they would work this time, and drafted a message to send that would make them reach back out to you.

You started to think about it all—deeply … very very deeply. Days passed by. You had hoped they would have contacted you by now, but they had not.

*"Maybe I'm supposed to be doing something different here."*

In the time that you had not been in communication with them, you realized something new about yourself. You were at peace and no longer felt like you had to come up with the solutions to drive the relationship forward.

You had not felt this way in years, maybe never in your life. You decided to trust that this feeling of peace would lead you in the right direction, and took a step forward.

In this moment, you made the decision to make yourself the priority and to shower yourself with all the love and affection that you had been giving so freely to others. You started to ask yourself new questions.

> *What will make me happy today?*
>
> *How can I spend my time off work to bring myself peace and joy?*
>
> *Who am I becoming now that I am making myself a priority and meeting my own needs?*
>
> *What needs do I have that still need to be met?*

One of your biggest issues was neglecting yourself in order to meet the needs of others. If someone were to ask you about what you needed, you probably would not have known what to say to them. *"You mean, I have needs? I thought that was something that everyone else had but me. I have no idea what I need."*

You've been given the opportunity for deep introspection, both to determine what your needs are and how you need to meet them. You are starting to shower yourself with all the love and affection that you were once only giving to others.

At several points in your life, you have felt broken and unworthy of the love that you so easily and graciously provided to others.

You wondered if you would ever be able to feel the way you made them feel.

You wondered what life would look like if you received the deep love that you had been searching for for so long. Then, when you least expected it, the deep and unwavering love that you had hoped for showed up on your doorstep in the form of self-love. The day that you finally made the choice to make yourself a priority, the path to self-love began.

By taking a risk on this part of your journey, you learned who you are, what you need, and how to meet those needs daily. This has not been an easy process for you, because you were so disconnected from the woman you once were.

Life has challenged you, but your love has transcended you and helped you to finally see how beautiful you really are—flaws and all. Now, settling for anything less than you deserve is a thing of the past.

Wherever you are on your healing journey, you are always worthy of love. Please continue to be patient, kind, and loving to yourself even when you do not feel like you deserve it.

When you show yourself compassion, you begin to heal in ways you never thought possible, opening doors to inner peace and self-acceptance. You deserve the same unwavering, open-heart love that you always give so freely to others.

Make sure that you are giving it to yourself on a daily basis and allowing it to cover you like a warm, soft blanket on a cold and snowy winter's day. You are worthy of the love that you desire.

## Actionable Step

This actionable step may require a little more thinking on your part, especially if you are still giving love so freely to others while not keeping any for yourself.

Create a self-love ritual. This could be as simple as writing down things you love about yourself each day, or treating yourself with kindness and care.

Be patient and trust your process. Remember, this journey is unique to you.

# 20 | LIVING IN YOUR POWER: EMBRACING YOUR FUTURE WITH GRACE

*"You have the power to change your thoughts and your thoughts have the power to change your life."*

—Ron Willingham

You've spent so much of your life living in survival mode, holding onto whatever fragments of control you could find. You have always been powerful, but kept it buried under the weight of trauma, fear, and self-doubt.

What if, instead of just surviving, you decided to truly live in your power?

Imagine waking up each day knowing that you, as the author of your story, are no longer held back by the shadows of your past, and capable of moving forward with grace and purpose. Embracing your future is not just about healing—it's about stepping fully into who you are meant to be, reclaiming every part of yourself, and walking boldly toward the life you deserve.

Your life has been a mixed bag of ups, downs, and complete turnarounds. You have often wondered how you would ever make things work so you could live in peace and experience true happiness.

You have faced the majority of your battles alone. During those times, you were able to find solace in your own voice and in your journey. In your darkest moments, life continues to unfold for you even when you are sitting silently.

The way you have felt—broken, discarded, unloved, and unworthy—has made it easy for you to provide abundant love, grace, peace, and kindness to others, as you would not wish on anyone to feel that way.

You have experienced a deep ache within your heart that no one could fix, and cried more tears than you are able to count. You thought that you would remain broken and unworthy of everything you desire forever.

You thought you'd never have an open-heart type of love that is true and everlasting, a deep and genuine connection with a supportive counterpart who just seems to *get* you even when you do not understand yourself.

Everything that you have worked so hard to achieve sometimes feels like it has fallen on deaf ears and blind eyes. You constantly question if your dreams would ever become a part of your reality.

*"I have done so much work. I just don't see things happening for me."*

Sometimes when you look for something for so long, it escapes you. It feels like when you search the couch for your keys ten times without finding them, only to finally spot them when you go back one more time. Or when you have searched the house for your glasses, frustrated and annoyed, only to realize they were sitting on your head the entire time. You get so angry with yourself that you can't even laugh at what just occurred. It's almost like playing hide and seek with yourself.

Then there are those moments that will warm your heart forever, when you catch complete brilliance. Like seeing your older children standing together at the door looking outside, and suddenly being reminded of when they were younger.

The mornings that you walk outside with your coffee to smell the crisp fall air, without experiencing any fear at all. The times when you journal your thoughts in the bathtub so you feel completely free and unapologetically you. These are the moments that help you redefine life based on your own terms, instead of someone else's.

Living in your power means living with strength, resilience, and making choices that are right by your heart and crafted by your mind. These choices have been some of the most difficult choices you have ever had to make—like letting go of everything that was toxic to your soul, even though it made you comfortable. Walking away from an abusive relationship even though you still cared about them. Divorcing an individual who made you question your self-worth. Saying goodbye to a job that's familiar but doesn't feed your soul. Creating a new and empowering environment for you and your kids to thrive in. Embrace things you've never tried.

While your life may not have always been the easiest, you made it work to the best of your ability. You've paved your own way forward multiple times, with your willingness to step up and come up with out-of-the-box solutions to handle the hard things in life. Not everyone could have handled all of this change, discomfort, and uncertainty—but you did.

You have shown great bravery in the ways you tackle life and embrace the hard times, especially when others have counted you out. In the darkest of moments, even when it felt like you did not matter, you showed yourself that you did by providing yourself with nurturing and loving care.

By creating and implementing healthy boundaries in your relationships, you stopped forcing yourself to show up for others when they were not willing to do the same for you.

Each day you wake up with the ability to make new, different decisions than the ones that you made before. In doing this, you welcome vast opportunities that you never thought you would experience.

You have created a new path to an emotionally satisfying career, made a house into a home, and provided yourself with a safe space to heal and grow into the best version of yourself.

Living in your power means being unapologetically you, even doing things others would choose not to do.

During the times when you were questioning everything, you were actually setting things into motion. Not enough time had occurred yet, so you could not see the seeds of growth you were planting along the way as they bloomed into the greatest part of your story.

For years, you handed the pen over to others and allowed them to write your story while you patiently waited your turn. Once you realized the stories that others were writing about you had nothing to do with who you truly were, you decided to ditch their narratives and create your own.

Now, the story that you are creating accurately matches the woman it is portraying. This story is about a woman who has risked everything, and come out more empowered and enlightened than she ever thought was possible.

In this space, you can become who you were always meant to be. Even when life has had you on bended knee, you have chosen to stay and plead. Put the pen to paper, and finally allow yourself to be free. We have arrived at our next actionable step with great glee.

## Actionable Step

Write a vision statement for your future. Include how you will continue to live in your power and what you hope to achieve moving forward.

Every day is a fresh start to live the life that you have always envisioned for yourself. Remember to always be kind, patient, and loving to yourself, and that it's completely ok to make changes as you go. Nothing is concrete unless you choose to make it so.

Life will unfold for you in ways that you never imagined. Embrace the journey and allow it to be uniquely, unapologetically yours. Celebrate yourself in small ways every day, because you are brilliant, beautiful, and deserving.

Please feel free to connect with me at any time on your journey. I would love to hear from you and learn more about your experiences. Please reach out to me via email at gina@ginahamiltoncoaching.com.

# A NOTE FROM ME TO *YOU*

As you turn the final page of *Healing Beyond the Hurt: Turning Trauma into Triumph*, take a moment to reflect on the remarkable journey you've been on. From the early chapters where we first touched the rawness of your pain, to now, where you stand stronger, braver, and more determined to embrace the life that is rightfully yours.

You've revisited wounds you thought were long buried, cried tears you've held back for too long, and faced the memories that once held you captive. There were moments of doubt, times when the weight of it all felt too much, yet here you are—still standing.

We began with boundaries and learning how to build those bridges of safety and connection, both within yourself and with the world around you. You then explored the sacred art of self-care, discovering how nourishing your mind, body, and soul becomes an act of rebellion and self-love. The path to peace, forgiveness, and letting go opened doors to emotional freedom, while empathy taught you the importance of meeting yourself and others with compassion.

You've rewritten your narrative, no longer seeing yourself as a victim of circumstance but as the hero of your own story. You've found your voice, learned to speak your truth, and embraced the art of letting go, allowing you to rise like a phoenix from the ashes.

You've transformed scars into stars, learning that even the darkest parts of your past can be sources of light, strength, and wisdom.

Each chapter has asked something of you: to dig deeper, to trust the process, and most importantly, to believe in your own capacity to heal. And you have. You've done the hard work—reflecting, unlearning, and transforming. You've allowed yourself to evolve into a version of yourself that is unbroken, empowered, and free.

But this is just the beginning. Triumph is not an endpoint; it's a continuous journey. You've stepped into your power, and now, it's time to keep moving forward with grace, confidence, and the knowledge that you are deserving of all the beauty life has to offer. The path ahead may still have its challenges, but you have proven to yourself that you can navigate anything that comes your way.

So, celebrate this moment. Celebrate your strength, your resilience, and your unwavering dedication to healing. You have done what many cannot, and that deserves to be honored. Take pride in the fact that you are becoming exactly who you were always meant to be—a woman of triumph. Keep going, because this new chapter of your life, the one you are writing for yourself, is full of possibility, joy, and peace. You are no longer defined by your pain, but by your power.

Let's take one more actionable step together.

Reflect on your journey through this book. Write down the most significant change you've experienced and how you plan to continue your healing journey.

## ACKNOWLEDGMENTS

*I* would like to take a moment and thank my dad, who passed away in 2013. For all the times that you provided a safe space to speak my truth, the acceptance that you provided during the times that I embarked on something quite different than the normal, and for taking the time to sit with me while I cried and showing me that there is an unconditional love that is truly fulfilling to the heart and soul. I learned how to be a parent because of your love for me, and I am grateful to pass that same love on to my sons. You are missed daily.

I want to thank all of my furry, four-legged loves of my life who provided me with unconditional love and support during my journey, sat with me when I cried, and protected me when I struggled. I love all of you immensely.

I want to thank the experiences of my life that have led me to become the person who I was always meant to be. If those situations and circumstances would not have happened, I may not have chosen to believe in myself a little more, and trust in my abilities to create new pathways that have brought me a beautiful beginning repeatedly.

I'm more than grateful to have my editing team and publisher by my side during this new endeavor. Lori Lynn, Nick Cunningham, and Shanda Trofe, thank you for making this a positive experience that has been rewarding in every way imaginable … and beyond.

I want to thank all the mentors and guides that have helped me on my healing journey along the way. Your words, healing touch, and gentle smiles and guidance helped me in more ways than you could have ever imagined.

Thank you to all of my patients and their families who trusted in me to be a part of their journeys and allowed me to provide the support and caring concern that was needed during some of the toughest times of their lives. I am a much better health care provider because of you.

# ABOUT THE AUTHOR

*G*ina Marie Hamilton's journey, much like the journeys of those she seeks to help, has been marked by moments of profound pain, deep reflection, and an unwavering commitment to reclaiming her life.

She knows what it feels like to be shattered by trauma, to live in the shadow of fear, and to wonder if she would ever feel whole again. But, she also knows the power of transformation—the incredible strength that lies within us all, waiting to be uncovered, nurtured, and celebrated.

Gina has walked through the fire of trauma and emerged stronger, more resilient, and deeply committed to helping others do the same. Her life's work is dedicated to empowering women to overcome the obstacles that have held them back, to rediscover their worth, and to create lives filled with safety, confidence, happiness, and health.

As a health and wellness coach, podcaster, and advocate for women's empowerment, Gina focuses on those who have endured and survived trauma. Her own experiences have shaped her approach, allowing her to bring both professional expertise and personal understanding to every page of this book.

She has spent years studying, practicing, and teaching methods of healing that are not just effective but transformative. Gina's approach is rooted in empathy, warmth, and unconditional love because she knows that true healing happens when people feel seen, heard, and valued.

In addition to her coaching practice, Gina is an avid weightlifter and a single mom to identical twin boys who inspire her every day to be strong and resilient. Her background in the medical field has given her a deep understanding of the mind-body connection, which she integrates into her work with clients. But beyond the titles and accomplishments, Gina is a survivor—someone who has turned pain into power, fear into confidence, and trauma into triumph.

Gina is also the host of the podcast *Triumphant Over Trauma: Living Life Victoriously After Trauma*, available on all podcast platforms. This podcast dives deep into the stories of survival and resilience, offering practical advice, inspiration, and hope to listeners who are navigating their own healing journeys. She also shares daily content on her Facebook account, (gina.m.hamilton.5), and her Instagram page, (blueeyedqtpi), where she offers insights, encouragement, and community for those on the path to healing.

For those looking to dive even deeper, Gina's course, *Finding Direction from Within,* guides women with a history of trauma to explore self-discovery and transformation while cultivating self-confidence, self-love, and peace of mind. To learn more about this course, please visit the Self Love Store at:

**www.bodyelementsmindelevation.com/store**

To stay connected and learn more about Gina's work, you can follow her on social media or reach out directly via email at gina@ginahamiltoncoaching.com.

# STEP INTO YOUR POWER

Picture yourself at a crossroads. Behind you lies the weight of past trauma, each memory a stone in the pack you've carried for too long. Ahead, a path emerges through the fog, leading to a life where you stand tall, radiant, and free. That path begins here.

As a companion to *Healing Beyond the Hurt*, the **Finding Direction from Within** course transforms the insights from this book into actionable steps. Consider it your personal compass for navigating the complexities of healing. Where the book illuminates the journey, the course provides the map and tools to walk it.

**Finding Direction from Within** meets you where you are and guides you forward. Through carefully crafted modules, you'll discover how to transform pain into fuel for growth, replace self-doubt with confidence, and build boundaries that protect your peace. This course becomes your lifeline, connecting you to the strength that already exists within you.

You'll develop:

- A personalized self-care routine that addresses both mental and emotional healing
- Clear, achievable goals that create lasting transformation

- New perspectives that help you rewrite your story and claim your power

The future you envision, where trauma no longer defines you, begins with this next step.

**Continue your journey at:**
**www.bodyelementsmindelevation.com/store**

## CONNECT WITH GINA

- facebook.com/gina.m.hamilton.5
- instagram.com/blueeyedqtpi
- triumphantovertraumalivinglifevictoriouslyaftertrauma.buzzsprout.com
- bodyelementsmindelevation.com

www.ingramcontent.com/pod-product-compliance
Lightning Source LLC
LaVergne TN
LVHW010329070526
838199LV00065B/5692